Simply Cheesecake

Over 90 Delicious Cheesecake Recipes From Around The World

Sue Fields

Editor: Jillian Alston
Cover Design: Aris Lukas

First Printing, 2010

ISBN 1450564585

Printed in the United States of America

Table of Contents

A Brief Cheesecake History

Before we dive into the recipes, I wanted to start with a short history of cheesecake just because I find the history of "how a food came to be" fascinating, and maybe some of you may find it interesting as well. And trust me, this truly is a "brief history."

Cheesecake supposedly originated in Ancient Greece. One of the first recorded "mentionings" of cheesecakes reports cheesecakes were served to Olympic athletes during the first Olympics in 776 B.C.

Along with the Roman conquest of Greece, the cheesecake "secret" fell into Roman hands. The Romans began calling this type of cake "placenta," (which happens to be from a Greek term). Placenta was more like a "cake of cheese," baked on a base of pastry or inside of a pastry "pocket." The Romans also called these cakes "libum," and they were often used as an offering at their temples to their gods.

230 A.D. - The first ingredients and recipe for cheesecakes were recorded by Atnenaeus, a Greek writer--This according to John J. Sergeto, author of Cheesecake Madness.

1000 A.D. - The introduction of cheesecake to Great Britain and Western Europe by the Roman conquering armies. By 1000 A.D., cheesecakes were practically everywhere throughout Scandinavia, England, and northwestern Europe.

1545- A recipe for "cheesecake" appears in an actual cookbook!

1872 - American dairymen, in attempting to duplicate the popular Neufchatel cheese of France, discovered a formula for an un-ripened cheese that was even richer and creamier. They called it cream cheese.

Cultures all over the world, past and present, have loved a tasty cheesecake. Culinary historians report cheesecake recipes dating back to the first century AD, with additional recipes from the centuries that followed. Cheesecake recipes exist today with every imaginable topping and flavor, but baking creamy cheese with sweetener has been around since almost (very almost) the beginning of time!

Present Day - Some extra-magnificently magically delicious "Cheesecake" Recipes arrive, almost mysteriously delivered into your hands.

Now that you know the background, enjoy these spectacular Cheesecake recipes.

Chocolate Velvet Cheesecake

Ingredients:
- ☐ 1 c Vanilla Wafer Crumbs
- ☐ 1/2 c Chopped Pecans
- ☐ 3 tb Granulated Sugar
- ☐ 1/4 c Margarine, Melted
- ☐ 16 oz Cream Cheese, Softened
- ☐ 1/2 c Brown Sugar, Packed
- ☐ 2 ea Large Eggs
- ☐ 6 oz Semi-sweet Chips, Melted
- ☐ 3 tb Almond Flavored Liqueur
- ☐ 2 c Sour Cream
- ☐ 2 tb Granulated Sugar

Directions:
Combine crumbs, pecans, granulated sugar and margarine; press onto bottom of 9-inch springform pan. Bake at 325 degrees F., 10 minutes. Combine cream cheese and brown sugar, mixing at medium speed on electric mixer until well blended.

Add eggs, one at a time, mixing well after each addition. Blend in chocolate and liqueur; pour over crust. Bake at 325 degrees F., 35 minutes. Increase oven temperature to 425 degrees F. Combine sour cream and granulated sugar; carefully spread over cheesecake.

Bake at 425 degrees F. 10 minutes. Loosen cake from rim of pan; cool before removing rim of pan. Chill.

VARIATION: Substitute 2 Tablespoons milk and 1/4 teaspoon almond extract for almond flavored liqueur.

Cookies and Cream Cheesecake

Ingredients:
- ☐ 2 c Cream-filled Cookies *
- ☐ 6 tb Margarine, Softened
- ☐ 1 ea Env. Unflavored Gelatin
- ☐ 1/4 c Cold Water
- ☐ 8 oz Cream Cheese Softened
- ☐ 1/2 c Sugar
- ☐ 3/4 c Milk
- ☐ 1 c Whipping Cream, Whipped
- ☐ 1 1/4 c Creme-filled Cookies **

Directions:

* The cookies (24) should be chocolate cream filled cookies and be to as fine as can be done.

** These cookies should be chocolate cream filled cookies and should be coarsely chopped.

Combine cookie crumbs and margarine; press onto bottom of 9-inch springform pan. Soften gelatin in water; stir over low heat until dissolved. Combine cream cheese and sugar, mixing at medium speed on an electric mixer until well blended.

Gradually add gelatin mixture and milk, mixing until well blended. Chill until mixture is thickened but not set. Fold in whipped cream. Reserve 1 1/2 C cream cheese mixture; pour remaining cream cheese mixture over crust. Top with cookies and reserved cream cheese mixture. Chill until firm.

Creamy Chilled Cheesecake

Ingredients:
- ☐ 1 c Graham Cracker Crumbs
- ☐ 1/4 c Sugar
- ☐ 1/4 c Margarine, Melted
- ☐ 1 ea Env. Unflavored Gelatin
- ☐ 1/4 c Cold Water
- ☐ 8 oz Cream Cheese, Softened
- ☐ 1/2 c Sugar
- ☐ 3/4 c Milk
- ☐ 1/4 c Lemon Juice
- ☐ 1 c Shipping Cream, Whipped
- ☐ 1 x Strawberry Halves

Directions:
Combine Crumbs, sugar, and margarine; press onto bottom of 9-inch spring- form pan.

Soften gelatin in water; stir over low heat until dissolved. Combine cream cheese and sugar, mixing at medium speed on electric mixer until well blended.

Chill until slightly thickened; fold in whipped cream. Pour over crust; chill until firm. Top with strawberries before serving.

Chocolate Raspberry Cheesecake

Ingredients:
- ☐ 1 1/2 c Creme-filled Cookie Crumbs *
- ☐ 2 tb Margarine, Melted
- ☐ 32 oz Cream Cheese, Softened
- ☐ 1 1/4 c Sugar
- ☐ 3 ea Large Eggs
- ☐ 1 c Sour Cream
- ☐ 1 ts Vanilla
- ☐ 6 oz Semi-sweet Chocolate Chips**
- ☐ 1/3 c Strained Raspberry Preserves
- ☐ 6 oz Semi-sweet Chocolate Chips
- ☐ 1/4 c Whipping Cream

Directions:
* Cookie crumbs should come from 18 Cream Filled Cookies that have been finely crushed.

** This 6 ozs of Chocolate chips should be melted and cooled slightly.

Combine crumbs and margarine; press onto bottom of 9-inch springform pan. Combine 24 ozs of cream cheese and sugar, mixing at medium speed on electric mixer until well blended.

Add eggs, one at a time, beating well after each addition. Blend in sour cream and vanilla; pour over crust. Combine remaining 8 ozs cream cheese and melted chocolate, mixing at medium speed on electric mixer until well blended.

Add Red Raspberry preserves; mix well. Drop rounded measuring tablespoonfuls of chocolate cream cheese batter over plain cream cheese batter, do not swirl. Bake at 325 degrees F., 1 hour and 25 minutes.

Loosen cake from rim of pan; cool before removing rim of pan. Melt chocolate pieces and whipping cream over low heat stirring until smooth. Spread over cheescake.

Chill. Garnish with additional whipping cream, whipped, raspberries and fresh mint leaves, if desired.

Arizona Sunset Cheesecake

Ingredients:

Shortbread Crust
- ☐ 1 1/2 c Flour
- ☐ 1/2 c Finely ground pecans
- ☐ 1/3 c Sugar
- ☐ 1 large Egg, separated
- ☐ 1/2 c Butter, softened

Cranberry Glaze Filling
- ☐ 1 cn Whole berry cranberry- sauce OR 2 cups cranberry orange relish
- ☐ 2 tb Sugar
- ☐ 1 tb Cornstarch
- ☐ 1 tb Grated lemon zest
- ☐ 1 tb Lemon juice

White Chocolate Filling
- ☐ 1 1/2 c Fresh orange juice
- ☐ 1-3 Inch x 1 inch piece- of orange peel (orange part only)
- ☐ 4 8 oz pkgs cream cheese
- ☐ 2/3 c Sugar
- ☐ 1 tb Grated orange zest
- ☐ 2 tb Cranberry Liqueur (such- as Crantasia Schnapps)
- ☐ 8 oz White chocolate, melted
- ☐ 4 Eggs

Candied Orange Topping
- ☐ 4 c Water
- ☐ 2 c Sugar
- ☐ 3 Seedless oranges (unpeeled)- cut into paper-thin slices
- ☐ **Garnish**
- ☐ **Whipped Cream**

Directions:
Shortbread Crust: Preheat the oven to 400 degrees
F. Working on a large flat surface, such as a
pastry board, place flour, pecans, and sugar in the
center of the surface and mix together.

Form a small depression or well in the center of
the mound. Add the egg yolk and the softened
butter to the well, then blend these with the dry
mixture. Mix the ingredients thoroughly using
your hands -- there is no substitute for warm
hands.

Shape the dough into a ball and wrap in plastic
wrap. Chill for at least 10 minutes. Roll out the
dough to a thickness of about 1/4-inch. You
should have a circle of about 11 inches in
diameter. For best results, roll out your dough
between 2 sheets of waxed paper, then peel away
the paper and cut the crust in a 9 inch circle.
Place the circle inside a 9 inch springform pan.

Prick the crust several times with a fork to keep
the crust from puffing up during the baking. Place
the springform pan in the oven and bake for 15 to
20 minutes, or until light brown. Allow to cool.
Using the leftover dough, line the sides of the
springform pan.

Press the dough against the sides of the pan,
smoothing it so as to have a continuous layer of
crust all the way around the sides of the pan.
Make sure that the side crust meets the bottom
crust all the way around. Brush the reserved egg
white onto the shell, covering the bottom and

sides. This will seal the dough and keep it from becoming soggy. Set aside until ready to use.

Cranberry Glaze Filling: Mix the sugar and cornstarch together in a small saucepan. Stir in the cranberry sauce. Cook over medium heat, stirring constantly, until thick. Stir in the lemon zest and lemon juice. Set aside to cool slightly.

White Chocolate Filling: Reset the oven to 350 degrees F. Boil the orange juice and piece of orange peel in a heavy medium saucepan until the juice is reduced to 3 Tbsp - about 12 minutes. Remove and discard the strip of orange peel and set aside the reduced orange juice. Using an electric mixer, beat the cream cheese, sugar, grated orange zest, Crantasia, and reduced orange juice until smooth.

Beat in the melted white chocolate and then the eggs, one at a time, beating just until combined. Pour the cranberry glaze filling into the prepared crust, spreading evenly. Pour the white chocolate filling over the cranberry layer and bake about 50 minutes (the top will be dry and the sides puffed slightly - the center will not be set). Move cheesecake to a wire rack and cool completely to room temperature. Chill in the refrigerator overnight.

Candied Oranges Topping: Cover a wire rack with waxed paper. Set aside. Combine the water and sugar in a heavy shallow wide skillet. Stir over medium heat until the sugar dissolves. Simmer 5 minutes longer. Add the orange slices 1 at a time and adjust the heat so that the syrup bubbles only around the edges of the pan. Cook the oranges for one hour. Turn over the top layer of oranges and cook until the oranges are translucent and the orange peels tender, about another one hour longer. Lift and drain each orange slice out of the syrup, and arrange the slices in a single layer on the prepared rack. Let dry 1 hour. Boil the orange-sugar syrup until thick, about 6 minutes. Loosen and remove the sides of the springform pan. Set the cheesecake on a serving dish. Overlap the candied orange slices around the top of the cheesecake. Reheat the orange syrup, if necessary, and brush over the orange slices. Drizzle any remainder over each serving. Garnish: whipped cream.

NOTE: You may substitute grapefruits for the oranges in the Candied Oranges Topping if you prefer.

Simply Cheesecake

Chocolate Chip Cheesecake Supreme

Ingredients:
- ☐ 1 c Chocolate Wafer Crumbs
- ☐ 3 tb Margarine, Melted
- ☐ 24 oz Cream Cheese, Softened
- ☐ 3/4 c Sugar
- ☐ 1/4 c Unbleached All-Purpose Flour
- ☐ 3 ea Large Eggs
- ☐ 1/2 c Sour Cream
- ☐ 1 ts Vanilla
- ☐ 1 c Mini Semi-sweet Chips

Directions:
Combine crumbs and margarine; press onto bottom of 9-inch springform pan. Bake at 350 degrees F., 10 minutes.

Combine cream cheese, sugar and flour, mixing at medium speed on electric mixer until well blended. Add eggs, one at a time, mixing well after each addition.

Blend in sour cream and vanilla. Stir in chocolate chips and pour into crust. Bake at 350 degrees F., 55 minutes. Loosen cake from rim of pan; cool before removing rim of pan.

Chill. Garnish with whipped cream and fresh mint leaves, if desired.

Cappuccino Cheesecake

Ingredients:
- ☐ 1 1/2 c Finely Chopped Nuts
- ☐ 2 tb Sugar
- ☐ 3 tb Margarine, Melted
- ☐ 32 oz Cream Cheese, Softened
- ☐ 1 c Sugar
- ☐ 3 tb Unbleached All-purpose Flour
- ☐ 4 ea Large Eggs
- ☐ 1 c Sour Cream
- ☐ 1 tb Instant Coffee Granules
- ☐ 1/4 ts Cinnamon
- ☐ 1/4 c Boiling water

Directions:
Combine nuts, sugar, and margarine; press onto bottom of 9-inch spring- form cake pan. Bake at 325 degrees F., 10 minutes.

Combine cream cheese, sugar, and flour, mixing at medium speed on electric mixer until well blended. Add eggs, one at a time, mixing well after each addition.

Blend in sour cream. Dissolve coffee granules and cinnamon in water. Cool; gradually add to cream cheese mixture, mixing until well blended. Pour over crust.

Bake at 450 degrees F., 10 minutes. Reduce oven temperature to 250 degrees F.; continue baking 1 hour. Loosen cake from rim of pan; cool before removing rim of pan.

Chill. Garnish with whipped cream and whole

coffee beans if desired.

Chocolate Mint Meringue Cheesecake

Ingredients:
- ☐ 1 c Chocolate Wafer Crumbs
- ☐ 3 tb Margarine, Melted
- ☐ 2 tb Sugar
- ☐ 24 oz Cream Cheese, Softened
- ☐ 2/3 c Sugar
- ☐ 3 ea Large Eggs
- ☐ 1 c Mint Chocolate Chips, Melted
- ☐ 1 ts Vanilla
- ☐ 3 ea Large Egg Whites
- ☐ 7 oz Marshmallow Creme (1 Jr)

Directions:
Combine crumbs, margarine and sugar; press onto bottom of 9-inch spring- form pan.

Bake at 350 degrees F., 10 minutes.

Combine cream cheese and sugar, mixing at medium speed on electric mixer until well blended. Add eggs, one at a time, mixing well after each addition.

Blend in mint chocolate and vanilla; pour over crust. Bake at 350 degrees F., 50 minutes. Loosen cake from rim of pan; cool before removing rim of pan.

Chill. Beat egg whites until soft peaks form. Gradually add marshmallow crème, beating until stiff peaks form. Carefully spread over top of cheesecake to seal.

Bake at 450 degrees F.; 3 to 4 minutes or until

lightly browned.

Cherry Cheesecake

Ingredients:
- ☐ 1 c Graham Cracker Crumbs
- ☐ 3 tb Sugar
- ☐ 3 tb Margarine, Melted
- ☐ 24 oz Cream Cheese, Softened
- ☐ 3/4 c Sugar
- ☐ 3 ea Large Eggs
- ☐ 1 ts Vanilla
- ☐ 21 oz Cherry Pie Filling (1 cn)

Directions:
Combine crumbs and margarine; press onto bottom of 9-inch springform pan.

Bake at 325 degrees F., 10 minutes.

Combine cream cheese and sugar, mixing at medium speed on electric mixer until well blended. Add eggs, one at a time mixing well after each addition.

Blend in vanilla; pour over crust. Bake at 450 degrees F., 10 minutes.

Reduce oven temperature to 250 degrees F., continue baking 25 to 30 minutes or until set. Loosen cake from rim of pan; cool before removing rim of pan.

Chill. Top with pie filling just before serving.

Chocolate Turtle Cheesecake

Ingredients:
- ☐ 2 c Vanilla Wafer Crumbs
- ☐ 6 tb Margarine, Melted
- ☐ 14 oz Carmels (1 bag)
- ☐ 5 oz (1 cn) Evaporated Milk
- ☐ 1 c Chopped Pecans, Toasted
- ☐ 16 oz Cream Cheese, Softened
- ☐ 1/2 c Sugar
- ☐ 1 ts Vanilla
- ☐ 2 ea Large Eggs
- ☐ 1/2 c Semi-sweet Chocolate Chips *

Directions:
* Chocolate chips should be melted.

Combine crumbs and margarine, press onto bottom and sides of 9-inch spring- form pan. Bake at 350 degrees F., 10 minutes.

In 1 1/2-quart heavy saucepan, melt caramels with milk over low heat, stirring frequently, until smooth. Pour over crust. Top with pecans.

Combine cream cheese, sugar and vanilla, mixing at medium speed on electric mixer until well blended. Add eggs, one at a time, mixing well after each addition.

Blend in chocolate, pour over pecans. Bake at 350 degrees F., 40 minutes. Loosen cake from rim of pan; cool before removing rim of pan.

Chill. Garnish with whipped cream, additional chopped nuts and maraschino cherries, if desired.

Chocolate Orange Supreme Cheesecake

Ingredients:
- ☐ 1 c Chocolate Wafer Crumbs
- ☐ 1/4 ts Cinnamon
- ☐ 3 tb Margarine, Melted
- ☐ 32 oz Cream Cheese, Softened
- ☐ 3/4 c Sugar
- ☐ 4 ea Large Eggs
- ☐ 1/2 c Sour Cream
- ☐ 1 ts Vanilla
- ☐ 1/2 c Semi-sweet Choc. ChipsMelted
- ☐ 2 tb Orange Flavord Liqueur
- ☐ 1/2 ts Grated Orange Peel

Directions:
Combine crumbs, cinnamon and margarine; press onto bottom of 9-inch spring- form pan.

Bake at 325 degrees F., 10 minutes.

Combine cream cheese and sugar, mixing at medium speed on electric mixer until well blended. Add eggs, one at a time, mixing well after each addition.

Blend in sour cream and vanilla. Blend chocolate into 3 cups batter; blend liqueur and pour into remaining batter. Pour chocolate batter over crust.

Bake at 350 degrees F., 30 minutes. Reduce oven temperature to 325 degrees F.

Spoon remaining batter over chocolate batter continue baking 30 minutes more.

Loosen cake from rim of pan; cool before removing rim of pan. Chill.

Cocoa-Nut Meringue Cheesecake

Ingredients:
- [ ] 7 oz (1 pk) Flaked Coconut *
- [ ] 1/4 c Chopped pecans
- [ ] 3 tb Margarine, Melted
- [ ] 16 oz Cream Cheese, Softened
- [ ] 1/3 c Sugar
- [ ] 3 tb Cocoa
- [ ] 2 tb Water
- [ ] 1 ts Vanilla
- [ ] 3 ea Large Eggs, Separated
- [ ] Dash salt
- [ ] 7 oz (1 jr) Marshmallow Creme
- [ ] 1/2 c Chopped Pecans

Directions:
* Coconut should be flaked and toasted.

Combine coconut, pecans, and margarine, press onto bottom of 9-inch springform pan.

Combine cream cheese, sugar, cocoa, water and vanilla, mixing at medium speed on electric mixer until well blended. Blend in egg yolks, pour over crust.

Bake at 350 degrees F., 30 minutes. Loosen cake from rim of pan, cool before removing rim of pan.

Beat egg whites and salt until foamy, gradually add marshmallow crème, beating until stiff peaks form. Sprinkle pecans over cheesecake to within 1/2-inch of outer edge.

Carefully spread marshmallow crème mixture over

top of cheescake to seal. Bake at 350 degrees F.,
15 minutes. Cool.

Tempting Trifle Cheesecake

Ingredients:
- ☐ 1 1/2 c Soft Coconut Macaroons*
- ☐ 3/4 c Sugar
- ☐ 1/2 c Whipping cream
- ☐ 2 tb Sweet Sherry
- ☐ 10 oz Red Raspberry Preserves
- ☐ 1 x Toasted Slivered Almonds
- ☐ 24 oz Cream Cheese, Softened
- ☐ 4 ea Large Eggs
- ☐ 1/2 c Sour Cream
- ☐ 1 ts Vanilla
- ☐ 1/2 c Whipping Cream, Whipped

Directions:
* Soft coconut macaroon cookies crumbs.

Press crumbs onto bottom of greased 9-inch springform pan. Bake at 325 degrees F., 15 minutes.

Combine cream cheese and sugar, mixing at medium speed on electric mixture until well blended. Add eggs, one at a time, mixing well after each addition.

Blend in sour cream, whipping cream, sherry and vanilla; pour over crust. Bake at 325 degrees F., 1 hour and 10 minutes.

Loosen cake from rim of pan; cool before removing rim of pan. Chill. Heat preserves in saucepan over low heat until melted.

Strain to remove seeds. Spoon over cheesecake,

spreading to edges. Dollop with whipped cream;
top with almonds.

Chocolate Cherry Cheesecake

Ingredients:
- ☐ 8 1/2 oz Chocolate Wafers, Fine Crush
- ☐ 1/2 c Butter, Melted
- ☐ 12 oz Semi-sweet Chocolate Chips
- ☐ 1 1/2 c Heavy cream
- ☐ 16 oz Cream Cheese, Softened
- ☐ 1/4 c Sugar
- ☐ 4 ea Large Eggs
- ☐ 3/4 c Cherry Flavored Liqueur
- ☐ 1 ts Vanilla Extract
- ☐ 1 lb Cherry Pie Filling
- ☐ 1/2 c Heavy Cream Whipped (Opt.)

Directions:
In large bowl, combine chocolate wafer crumbs and butter. Pat firmly into 9-inch springform pan, covering bottom and 2 1/2 inches up sides. Chill.

Preheat oven to 325 degrees F.

Combine over hot (not boiling) water, chocolate chips and heavy cream. Stir until morsels are melted and mixture is smooth. Set aside. In large bowl, combine cream cheese and sugar, beating until creamy.

Add eggs, one at a time, beating well after each addition. Add chocolate mixture, cherry liqueur, and vanilla, mix until blended. Pour into prepared crust.

Bake at 325 degrees F. for 60 minutes. Turn oven off. Let stand in oven with door ajar 1 hour. Remove, cool completely. Chill 24 hours.

Spread cherry pie filling over top of cheesecake leaving 1-inch from the edge. Decorate edge with whipped cream, if desired.

Tuscan Cheesecake

Ingredients:
- ☐ 3 lb Ricotta cheese
- ☐ 8 Eggs
- ☐ 2 c Sugar
- ☐ 1 c Milk
- ☐ 2 Oranges, grated zest only
- ☐ 2 Lemons, grated zest only
- ☐ 2 2/3 oz Grand mariner
- ☐ 1 tb Clarified butter
- ☐ 1/4 c Plain bread crumbs

Directions:
Preheat oven to 350 F.

Beat ricotta cheese with blender until smooth. Add eggs, sugar, and milk. Blend until well-mixed and smooth.

Add orange and lemon zest and Grand Mariner. Mix well.

Grease one cheesecake pan with butter and coat lightly with bread crumbs. Fill pan 3/4 of the way with cheesecake mixture.

Set pan in a larger pan filled half full with water and bake 1-1/4 hours. Turn oven off, leaving the cake within.

Let stand for one hour. Remove, let cool, and

refrigerate.

Another Chocolate Cheesecake

Ingredients:
- ☐ 1 pk (8 1/2 oz) chocolate wafers; crushed (Oreos work well, filling and all)
- ☐ 6 tb Unsalted butter; melted
- ☐ 2 pk (8 oz) cream cheese; softened (low fat works well)
- ☐ 2/3 c Sugar
- ☐ 3 Eggs
- ☐ 12 oz Or 2 cups semi-sweet chocolate, melted
- ☐ 1 c Whipping cream
- ☐ 2 tb Unsalted butter; melted
- ☐ 1 ts Vanilla
- ☐ 1/2 c Kahlua

Directions:
Heat oven to 325F.

In medium bowl, combine wafers and butter, reserving 1 tablespoon of the crumbs for garnish.

Press remaining crumbs in bottom and 2 inches up sides of an un-greased 10- inch springform pan. Refrigerate.

In a large bowl, combine cream cheese and sugar; beat until smooth. Add eggs 1 at a time, beating well after each addition. Add melted chocolate; beat well. Add remaining ingredients, and beat until smooth. Pour into crust-lined pan.

Bake at 325F for 55 to 65 minutes or until edges are set. Center of cheesecake will be soft. (To minimize cracking, place a shallow pan with about

3/4 inch of hot water on the lower oven rack while baking.)

Allow cheesecake to cool in the pan for 5 minutes, then carefully remove the sides of the pan.

Allow the cheesecake to cool completely. Garnish with the reserved crumbs (provided you can keep your spouse from eating them), and refrigerate (at least 2-3 hours, preferably overnight).

Keeps well in refrigerator for 3 days, probably longer.

Cheddar Chili Cheesecake

Ingredients:
- ☐ 1 1/2 tb Butter (for pan)
- ☐ 1/4 c Fine breadcrumbs, toasted
- ☐ 1/4 c Finely grated cheddar cheese
- ☐ 6 oz Thinly sliced ham
- ☐ 1 1/2 lb Cream cheese, room temp.
- ☐ 3/4 lb Sharp cheddar, grated
- ☐ 1 c Cottage cheese
- ☐ 3/4 c Chopped green onion
- ☐ 4 Eggs
- ☐ 3 tb Jalapeno pepper*
- ☐ 2 tb Milk
- ☐ 1 Garlic clove, halved .

Directions:
*seeded and finely chopped.

Preheat oven to 325.

Butter 9" springform pan.

Mix breadcrumbs and 1/4 cup cheddar. Sprinkle mixture into pan, turning to coat. Refrigerate.

Dice about half of ham; reserve remaining slices. Mix diced ham with remaining ingredients in blender or processor until smooth.

Pour slightly more than half of filling into prepared pan. Top with reserved ham slices in even layer. Cover with remaining filling. Set pan on baking sheet.

Bake 1 1/4 hours. Turn oven off and cool

cheesecake about 1 hour with door ajar. Transfer cheesecake to rack.

Cool to room temperature before serving.

Coconut Chocolate Cheesecake

Ingredients:
- ☐ 1 c Grham Cracker Crumbs
- ☐ 3 tb Sugar
- ☐ 3 tb Margarine, Melted
- ☐ 2 oz Unsweetened Baking Chocolate
- ☐ 2 tb Margarine
- ☐ 16 oz Cream Cheese, Softened
- ☐ 1 1/4 c Sugar
- ☐ 1/4 ts Salt
- ☐ 5 ea Large Eggs
- ☐ 1 1/3 c Flaked Coconut (3.5 oz Can)
- ☐ 1 c Sour Cream
- ☐ 2 tb Sugar
- ☐ 2 tb Brandy

Directions:
Combine crumbs, sugar and margarine; press onto bottom of 9-inch spring- form pan.

Bake at 350 degrees F., 10 minutes.

Melt chocolate and margarine over low heat; stirring until smooth. Combine cream cheese, sugar and salt; mixing at medium speed on electric mixer until well blended. Add eggs, one at a time, mixing well after each addition. Blend in chocolate mixture and coconut; pour over crust.

Bake at 350 degrees F., 55 to 60 minutes or until set.

Combine sour cream, sugar and brandy; spread over cheesecake. Bake at 300 degrees F., 5 minutes.

Loosen cake from rim of pan; cool before removing rim of pan. Chill.

Chocolate Cheesecake

Ingredients:
- ☐ 12 oz Semi-sweet chocolate; chopped
- ☐ 1 1/2 Sticks (3/4 cup) unsalted butter
- ☐ 1 c Sour cream at room temperature
- ☐ 1 ts Vanilla
- ☐ 3 lg Eggs
- ☐ 1 c Sugar
- ☐ 3 8-oz packages cream cheese; softened
- ☐ 1 c Chopped pecans
- ☐ Confectioners' sugar and unsweetened cocoa powder for dusting the cake if desired
- ☐ 1 Chocolate graham wafer pie crust

Directions:
In a large metal bowl set over a pan of barely simmering water melt the chocolate and the butter, stirring until the mixture is smooth, stir in the sour cream and the vanilla, and let the mixture cool.

In a bowl beat together the eggs and the sugar until the mixture is thick and pale and forms a ribbon when the beaters are lifted and beat in the cream cheese.

Stir in the chocolate mixture and fold in the pecans.

Pour the filling into the prepared crust and bake the cheesecake in the middle of a preheated 325 degree F oven for 2 hours, or until it is just set. (The cake will fall in the middle.)

Let the cheesecake cool in the pan on a rack, chill

it, covered loosely, overnight, and remove the side
of the pan. Sprinkle the confectioners' sugar and
the cocoa powder decoratively over the
cheesecake.

Banana Cream Cheesecake

Ingredients:
- ☐ 1 Yellow cake mix, prepared in 13x9 pan.
- ☐ 8 oz Cream cheese, room temperature
- ☐ 1 pk (3-oz) instant vanilla pudding
- ☐ 2 c Milk
- ☐ 3 Or 4 bananas
- ☐ 1 lg Container Cool Whip
- ☐ 1 c Chopped nuts

Directions:
Beat cream cheese until creamy. Add milk, gradually; add pudding, beating until well mixed.

Pour over cooled cake. Slice the bananas over cake.

Cover with Cool Whip and top with nuts.

A Masterpiece Cheesecake

Ingredients:
Crust:
- ☐ 2 C. graham cracker crumbs
- ☐ 1/4 C. melted butter
- ☐ 1/3 C. powdered sugar
- ☐ 2 Tbsp. flour

Directions:
Mix well and pat into greased 9" spring form pan (grease bottom of pan only).

Place in refrigerator while making filling.

Filling:
- ☐ 1 lb. cream cheese
- ☐ 3 eggs
- ☐ 1/2 C. sugar

Directions:
Beat well and pour into pie crust.

Bake in 350 degree F oven for 20 minutes ONLY.

Remove and cool.

Cake may be decorated with any variety of fruits, canned or in season.

Amaretto Peach Cheesecake

Ingredients:
- ☐ 3 tb Margarine
- ☐ 1/3 c Sugar
- ☐ 1 Large Egg
- ☐ 3/4 c Unbleached All-purpose Flour
- ☐ 24 oz Cream Cheese, Softened
- ☐ 3/4 c Sugar
- ☐ 3 tb Unbleached All-purpose Flour
- ☐ 3 Large Eggs
- ☐ 16 oz Canned Peach Halves *
- ☐ 1/4 c Almond Flavored Liqueur

Directions:
* Peach halves should be drained, and then pureed.

Combine margarine and sugar until light and fluffy. Blend in egg. Add flour; mix well. Spread dough onto bottom of 9-inch springform pan.

Bake at 450 degrees F., 10 minutes.

Combine cream cheese, sugar and flour; mixing at medium speed on electric mixer until well blended. Add eggs, one at a time, mixing well after each addition. Add peaches and liqueur; mix well. Pour over crust.

Bake at 450 degrees F., 10 minutes. Reduce oven temperature to 250 degrees F.; continue baking 65 minutes.

Loosen cake from rim of pan; cool before removing rim of pan. Chill.

Garnish with additional peach slices and sliced almonds, if desired.

Almond Amaretto Cheesecake

Ingredients:
Crust:
- [ ] 1/4 c Sugar
- [ ] 1/4 c Almonds, toasted
- [ ] 1 c Unsifted all-purpose flour
- [ ] Pinch salt
- [ ] 1/2 c Unsalt butter
- [ ] 1 lg Egg yolk
- [ ] 1/4 ts Almond extract

Filling:
- [ ] 5 pk Cream cheese, softened 8-oz each
- [ ] 1 2/3 c Sugar
- [ ] 2 ts Grated lemon zest
- [ ] 5 lg Eggs plus 2 yolks
- [ ] 1/4 c Heavy cream
- [ ] 3 tb Amaretto liqueur
- [ ] 1 tb All-purpose flour
- [ ] Strawberries for garnish

Directions:
Make Crust: Lightly greased 9-inch springform pan.

In food processor, process sugar and almonds until nuts are finely ground. Add flour and salt; pulse to blend.

Cut up butter into bits; add to flour mixture. Pulse until mixture resembles coarse crumbs. Add egg yolk and almond extract; pulse just until dough holds together.

Press dough into prepare pan to line bottom and 2 inch up sides. Refrigerate 1 hour.

Preheat oven to 400. Bake crust 8 minutes or just until golden. Place on wire rack; let stand until cool.

Make filling: In large bowl, with electric mixer at medium-high speed, beat cream cheese until light and fluffy.

Gradually beat in sugar; beat 3 minutes or until mixture is blended and smooth. Beat in lemon zest.

At medium speed, beat in eggs and yolks, on at a time, beating just until blended after each addition. At low speed, beat in heavy cream and liqueur. Beat in flour just until blended.

Increase oven temperature to 500. Pour filling into cooled crust in pan. Bake 12 minutes.

Reduce oven temperature to 200. Bake cheesecake 1 hour longer, cover loosely with foil if top browns too quickly.

Turn off oven; let cheesecake remain on rack for 30 minutes with oven door propped ajar with wooden spoon.

Place cake on cooling rack. Let stand until room temperature.

Cover; chill 6 hours or overnight.

To serve, run knife around edges of pan to loosen cake. Remove pan sides. Place cake on serving dish. Garnish with strawberries. Before cutting each slice, dip knife in cold water.

Simply Cheesecake

Cappuccino Cheesecake Pie with Pecan Sauce

Ingredients:
- ☐ 1 10" pie crust

Filling:
- ☐ 3 pk (8 oz) cream cheese; softened
- ☐ 1 3/4 c Firmly packed dark brown sugar
- ☐ 4 Eggs
- ☐ 2 tb Strong coffee

Sauce:
- ☐ 1 c Firmly packed dark brown sugar
- ☐ 1 c Whipping cream
- ☐ 1/2 c Butter
- ☐ 1/4 c Strong coffee
- ☐ 2 tb Coffee-flavored liqueur or strong coffee
- ☐ 1 c Pecan halves

Directions:
Heat oven to 350 degrees F.

In large bowl, beat cream cheese and 1 3/4 cups brown sugar until smooth. Add eggs; beat until well blended. Add 2 tbsps coffee; blend well. Pour into crust.

Bake at 350 degrees F for 45-50 minutes or until edges are set and golden brown (center will not appear set). Cover edge of crust with strips of foil after 15-20 minutes of baking to prevent excessive browning.

Cool, then refrigerate until thoroughly chilled and center is set, about 2 hours.

Simply Cheesecake

Sauce: In medium saucepan, combine all sauce ingredients except pecans. Bring to a boil over medium heat, stirring occasionally.

Reduce heat; simmer 5 minutes, stirring occasionally. Stir in 1 cup pecan halves.

To serve, pour warm sauce over each serving. Garnish with whipped cream and pecan halves.

Cheesecake

Ingredients:
Crust:
- ☐ 2 c Graham cracker crumbs
- ☐ 6 T Butter, melted
- ☐ 2 T Sugar, white
- ☐ 1/2 t Cinnamon, ground

Cake Filling:
- ☐ 1 1/2 lb Cream cheese
- ☐ 3/4 c Sugar
- ☐ 3 Eggs
- ☐ 1/4 c Lemon juice
- ☐ 2 t Lemon rind, grated
- ☐ 2 t Vanilla

Topping:
- ☐ 2 c Sour cream
- ☐ 3 T Sugar
- ☐ 1 T Vanilla

Glaze:
- ☐ 1/2 c Sugar
- ☐ 1 1/2 t Cornstarch
- ☐ 1/4 t Salt
- ☐ 3/4 c Water
- ☐ 1/3 c Lemon juice
- ☐ 1 Egg yolk, Well beaten
- ☐ 1 T Butter

Directions:
Preheat oven to 350 degrees F.

Combine crust ingredients. Press crust on bottom and sides of buttered 10-inch springform pan. Bake 5 minutes and cool.

Beat cheese until soft. Add sugar and blend well.

Add eggs, one at a time, beating well after each.

Mix in the lemon rind and the vanilla, and add to the mixture. Pour into the pre-baked crust and bake 35 minutes.

Combine topping ingredients, spread on top of cheesecake, and return to oven immediately. Bake 10-12 minutes and remove from oven.

 Combine dry glaze ingredients; add liquid glaze ingredients. Cook over low heat until thick. Add about 1 T of butter. Cool and spread this glaze on the cake before the glaze thickens too much.

Chocolate Amaretto Cheesecake

Ingredients:
- ☐ 1 1/2 c Chocolate wafer crumbs
- ☐ 1/3 c Heavy cream
- ☐ 1 c Blanched almonds, lightly toasted and chopped
- ☐ 1/2 c Amaretto
- ☐ 2 ts Vanilla
- ☐ 1/3 c Sugar
- ☐ 4 Eggs
- ☐ 6 tb Butter, softened
- ☐ 2 c Sour cream
- ☐ 24 oz Cream cheese, softened
- ☐ 1 tb Sugar
- ☐ 1 c Sugar
- ☐ 1 c Blanched almonds, lightly

Directions:
Preheat oven to 375.

Combine crumbs, almonds, sugar and butter. Pat mixture on bottom and sides of a 10 inch springform pan.

Cream together the cream cheese, sugar, heavy cream, liqueur, and 1 t vanilla. Beat in eggs, 1 at a beating well after each addition. Beat mixture until light.

Pour into crumb lined pan.

Bake in middle of oven for 1 1/2 hours or until top of cake cracks and knife inserted in middle comes out clean. Let stand on rack 5 minutes.

Simply Cheesecake

Combine sour cream, 1 t vanilla, and sugar. Mix well and spread evenly over cake.

Bake for 5 more minutes. Place on rack and let cool completely. cover lightly with wax paper and let chill overnight.

When ready to serve, remove sides from pan and garnish with toasted almonds around outer edge and on to of cake.

Diabetic Cheesecake

Ingredients:
- ☐ 6 Plain graham wafers - 2 1/2 x 2 1/2 inches each
- ☐ 1 1/2 tb Margarine, melted
- ☐ 1 tb Granulated gelatin
- ☐ 1/2 c Cold water
- ☐ 1/3 c Boiling water
- ☐ 1/2 ts Grated lemon rind
- ☐ 1/2 c Fresh lemon juice
- ☐ Sugar substitute equivalent to 1/4 cup sugar
- ☐ 2 tb Water
- ☐ 2 c (16 oz) cream-style cottage cheese 4% fat
- ☐ 1/2 ts Lemon extract
- ☐ 4 lg Strawberries

Directions:
Prepare an 8" x 8" x 2" cake pan with vegetable pan-coating; set aside.

Make fine crumbs, with graham crackers (1/2 cup) and mix thoroughly with melted margarine; set aside.

Soak gelatin in cold water. Combine boiling water and lemon rind; add to gelatin; add lemon juice and sweetener, stirring until completely dissolved.

Chill until it is the consistency of unbeaten egg whites. Put 2 tablespoons water, cottage cheese, and lemon extract into a blender or food processor and cover; turn to high speed for 10-15 seconds.

Add partially set gelatin mixture; turn to high

speed 15 seconds or until well blended. Pour into prepared pan.

Sprinkle graham cracker crumbs evenly over top. Wash, hull, and dry strawberries. Slice in halves lengthwise.

Arrange on top of cake so that, when cut into eight servings (4 by 2 inches), each will have a strawberry garnish in center.

Chill several hours, until set.

Chimpanzee Cheesecake

Ingredients:
Crust:
- ☐ 1 1/2 c Graham Cracker Crumbs
- ☐ 1/4 c Sugar; Granulated

Cheesecake
- ☐ 1 lb Cream Cheese
- ☐ 2 ts Lemon Juice
- ☐ 1 c Sour Cream
- ☐ 6 tb Melted Butter
- ☐ 1/4 c Granulated Sugar
- ☐ 4 Large Eggs
- ☐ 1 c Bananas Mashed *

Directions:
* Approximately 3 medium bananas should yield the 1 cup of mashed

Crust: Preheat the oven to 350 degrees F.

Place the crumbs in a mixing bowl and add the butter and sugar. Blend well. Press the crumb mixture onto the bottom and partly up the sides of a greased 9-inch springform pan.

Smooth the crumb mixture along the bottom to an even thickness. Bake for about 10 minutes in the oven at 350 degrees F. Cool before filling.

Cheesecake: Preheat the oven to 350 degrees F.

In a large mixing bowl, beat the cream cheese, sugar and lemon juice together. Add the eggs, one at a time, beating well after each addition.

Stir in the sour cream and the mashed bananas and blend well until very smooth.

Pour the mixture into the prepared crust and bake for 1 hour.

Cool in the oven, with the door propped open, until the cake is at room temperature. Chill until serving time.

7-Up Lemon Cheesecake with Strawberry Glaze

Ingredients:
Crumb Crust:
- ☐ 2 c Graham cracker crumbs
- ☐ 1/2 c Powdered sugar
- ☐ 1/2 c Butter; melted
- ☐ 1 ts Cinnamon

7-Up Filling
- ☐ 1 pk Unflavored gelatin
- ☐ 1 1/2 c 7-up
- ☐ 1 sm Lemon pudding & pie filling, not instant
- ☐ 6 tb Sugar
- ☐ 2 Eggs; beaten
- ☐ 3/4 c Water
- ☐ 11 oz Cream cheese; softened

Strawberry Glaze:
- ☐ 1/2 c Strawberry jelly; melted
- ☐ Fresh strawberries or unsweetened frozen, thawed whole strawberries

Directions:
Crust: Combine well the graham cracker crumbs, powdered sugar, cinnamon, and melted butter.

Press onto bottom and partway up sides of buttered 9" springform pan; chill.

Filling: Soften unflavored gelatin in 1/4 cup 7-up for 4 minutes. In a saucepan combine pie filling, sugar, beaten eggs and water. Blend well.

Add 1-1/4 cup 7-up and bring just to a boil over

medium heat stirring constantly; remove from
heat. Stir in softened gelatin; cool 3 minutes.

Add 1/2 cup of this warm mixture to softened
cream cheese; mash together. Mix together with
remaining 7-up mixture and stir until well
blended.

Turn into chilled crust and chill for at least 8
hours. Remove from pan and add topping.

Topping: Brush top of chilled cheesecake with
melted jelly. Arrange strawberries upright on cake
and spoon any remaining melted jelly over them.

8 Minute Cheesecake

Ingredients:
- ☐ 1 pk (8 oz.) cream cheese, softened
- ☐ 1/3 c Sugar
- ☐ 1 c (1/2 pt.) sour cream
- ☐ 2 ts Vanilla
- ☐ 1 (8 oz.) container Birds Eye Cool Whip whip
- ☐ 1 Keebler
- ☐ Fresh strawberries for garnish
- ☐ Ready Crust graham cracker pie crust

Directions:
Beat cheese until smooth; gradually beat in sugar.

Blend in sour cream and vanilla.

Fold in whipped topping, blending well. Spoon into crust.

Chill until set, at least 4 hours.

Garnish with fresh strawberries if desired.

Cherry Cheesecake

Ingredients:
Cheesecake:
- [ ] 2/3 c Cottage cheese
- [ ] Artificial sweetener; equal to 6 tb. sugar
- [ ] 1 tb Lemon; rind grated
- [ ] 1/2 ts Vanilla
- [ ] 2 Eggs; separated
- [ ] 1/4 c Evaporated skim milk
- [ ] 1/3 c Instant non-fat dry milk

Cherry Topping:
- [ ] 1 c Sweet cherries; pitted
- [ ] 1/4 c Cherry flavored beverage
- [ ] Artificial sweetener; to taste
- [ ] ¼ ts Cherry extract

Directions:
Cheesecake: Combine cottage cheese, sweetener, lemon rind, vanilla extract, egg yolks, evaporated milk and dry milk in a blender and blend for about 1 minute until well mixed.

Transfer to a bowl. In another bowl beat egg whites until they stand in stiff peaks; fold into the cheese mixture.

Transfer to springform pan and bake 40 minutes at 350 degrees F.

Topping: In a covered saucepan, cook cherries in beverage until they are tender and liquid is evaporated.

Sweeten, add extract, spread over baked cheesecake and return to oven 5 minutes more.

Simply Cheesecake

3-Step Blueberry Cheesecake

Ingredients:
- ☐ 2 pk 8 oz cream cheese
- ☐ 1/2 c Sugar
- ☐ 1/4 ts Vanilla
- ☐ 2 Eggs
- ☐ 1 9oz graham cracker crust
- ☐ 1 cn Blueberry pie filling

Directions:
Mix cream cheese, sugar, vanilla until smooth and creamy. Add eggs and mix well.

Pour into pie crust. Spoon 1/4 to 1/3 of pie filling on to top. Gently swirl with toothpick.

Bake at 350 degrees for 40 minutes or until center is set.

Cool to room temperature and then refrigerate.

Serve topped with remaining pie filling.

Chocolate Chip Cheesecake

Ingredients:
- ☐ Crust Bottom:
- ☐ 2 c Graham cracker crumbs
- ☐ 1/4 c Sugar
- ☐ 6 tb Butter, melted

Cake:
- ☐ 2 1/4 lb Cream Cheese
- ☐ 1 2/3 c Sugar
- ☐ 5 Eggs
- ☐ 1 c Bailey's Irish Cream
- ☐ 1 tb Vanilla Extract
- ☐ 1 c Semisweet Chocolate Chips

Topping:
- ☐ 1 c Whipping Cream
- ☐ 2 tb Sugar
- ☐ 1 ts Instant Coffee Powder

Garnish:
- ☐ Chocolate curls

Directions:
Preheat oven to 325 degrees.

Coat a 9" springform pan with nonstick vegetable spray. C

ombine crumbs and 1/4 cup of sugar in the pan and stir in the melted butter. Press mixture into bottom and 1 inch up the sides of the pan.

Bake until light brown, about 7 minutes.

In a food processor, beat cream cheese, add 1-2/3 cup sugar and eggs and mix. Blend in Bailey's and vanilla.

Sprinkle half of the chocolate chips over crust and spoon in filling. Sprinkle with remaining chocolate chips.

Bake cake until puffed, springy in center and golden brown, about 1 hour and 20 minutes. Cool cake completely.

Beat whipping cream, 2 tablespoons sugar and coffee powder until peaks form.

Spread mixture over cooled cake and garnish with chocolate curls.

Serves 12 to 15.

Cheesecake with Cranberry Jewel Topping

Ingredients:
- ☐ 1 1/2 c Vanilla wafers, crushed
- ☐ 1/4 c Sugar
- ☐ 6 tb Butter; melted

Filling:
- ☐ 1/2 c Whipping cream
- ☐ 1 pk Vanilla powder
- ☐ 1 1/2 lb Cream cheese; room temp.
- ☐ 1 c Sugar
- ☐ 1 pn Salt
- ☐ 4 lg Eggs

Topping:
- ☐ 12 oz Fresh or frozen cranberries
- ☐ 3/4 c Sugar
- ☐ 1/2 c Cranberry juice concentrate
- ☐ 1/4 c Water

Directions:
Preheat oven to 350 F.

Crust: Wrap the bottom and outsides of 9-inch springform pan with aluminum foil. Lightly butter inside of pan and set aside.

Combine cookie crumbs, sugar and butter. Press mixture onto bottom and halfway up sides of prepared springform pan.

Bake for 10 minutes on center rack of preheated oven. Set aside, but do not turn off oven.

Filling: Using electric mixer, blend together all

ingredients. Add eggs and mix just until well-combined. Pour filling into prepared crust.

Bake until center is just set, about 50 minutes. Refrigerate cake immediately, and leave until thoroughly chilled (at least 6 hours or overnight).

Topping: Combine all ingredients in heavy medium saucepan. Stir over medium heat until sugar is dissolved.

Bring to a boil and continue cooking for 3 minutes. Strain mixture through a sieve set over a large bowl, pressing firmly with the back of a spoon to force as much of the liquid through sieve as possible.

Spoon warm topping evenly over cold cake.

Refrigerate until topping is set, at least 2 hours. (Can be prepared 1 day before serving. Store covered in refrigerator.)

To serve, pipe rosettes of whipped cream around edges of cake. Garnish with whole cranberries.

Simply Cheesecake

Amaretto & Ghirardelli Chocolate Chip Cheesecake

Ingredients:
Crust:
- ☐ 1 c Ghirardelli semi-sweet chocolate chips
- ☐ 1 tb Butter, unsalted
- ☐ 1 1/4 c Vanilla wafer crumbs
- ☐ 1/4 c Nuts; finely chopped
- ☐ 3 tb Sugar, confectioners'

Filling:
- ☐ 24 oz Cream cheese; softened
- ☐ 1 c Sugar
- ☐ 4 lg Egg; room temp
- ☐ 1/4 c Amaretto
- ☐ 2 tb Cornstarch
- ☐ 1 ts Vanilla extract
- ☐ 1 c Ghirardelli semi-sweet chocolate chips

Topping:
- ☐ 2 c Sour cream; room temp
- ☐ 1/4 c Sugar
- ☐ 1 ts Amaretto
- ☐ 1/2 c Almonds, toasted sliced

Directions:
Make the crust: Position a rack in the center of the oven and preheat to 375 degrees F.

Lightly butter the bottom and side of a 9 x 3" round springform pan.

Trim a 9" cardboard cake circle so that it fits snugly within the curved lip of the bottom of the springform pan.

Cover the top of the cardboard lined springform bottom with a piece of aluminum foil, leaving a 2" overhang all the way around the edge.

Carefully attach the side of the springform so as not to tear the foil. Wrap the foil overhang halfway up the side of the springform pan.

Lightly butter the foil covered bottom and side of the springform pan.

In the top of a double boiler over hot, not simmering, water, melt the chocolate chips with the butter, stirring frequently, until smooth.

Remove the top part of the double boiler from the bottom and cool the chocolate mixture until tepid. In a large bowl, stir together the crumbs, nuts and sugar until combined. Add the chocolate mixture and using a fork, stir together the chocolate and crumbs, until combined.

Press the mixture evenly into the bottom of the prepared pan, making sure that the crust extends 1" up the side of the pan. Set aside.

Make the filling: In a large bowl, using a hand held electric mixer set at medium high speed, beat the cream cheese with the sugar for 2 to 3 minutes, or until smooth.

One at a time, beat in the eggs, beating well after each addition. Beat in the liqueur, cornstarch and vanilla until smooth. Stir in the chocolate chips.

Pour the cheesecake filling into the prepared pan and smooth the surface with a rubber spatula. Bake the cheesecake for 50 to 60 minutes, or until a knife comes out clean when inserted near the center. Cool for 5 minutes. Do not turn off the oven.

Make the topping: In a large bowl, stir together the sour cream, sugar and liqueur until combined and spread it evenly over the surface of the cake. Bake for 5 minutes longer.

Cool the cheesecake completely on a wire rack. Cover with plastic wrap and refrigerate overnight.

Remove the side of the pan and sprinkle the top with the almonds.

Brooklyn Cheesecake

Ingredients:
- ☐ 16 oz Ricotta cheese
- ☐ 16 oz Cream cheese, softened
- ☐ 1 1/2 c Sugar
- ☐ 4 Eggs
- ☐ Juice of 1/2 fresh lemon
- ☐ 1/4 t Vanilla
- ☐ 3 tb Cornstarch
- ☐ 3 tb Flour
- ☐ 1/4 c Melted butter
- ☐ 16 oz Sour cream

Directions:
Blend together ricotta and cream cheese, and add sugar. Beat in eggs, one at a time. Add lemon juice, vanilla, cornstarch, flour and butter. Mix well.

Fold in sour cream and pour into buttered 10-inch springform pan.

Put cake in a cold oven. Heat to 325 degrees, and bake for one hour.

Turn oven off and leave cake in for two more hours. Do not open oven door while cooling.

Remove cake and finish cooling. Wrap and refrigerate. Cake is best the next day.

No Bake Cheesecake

Ingredients:
- ☐ Graham cracker crust
- ☐ 1 1/4 lb Cream cheese, room temp.
- ☐ 1 1/2 ts Vanilla
- ☐ 1 c Sugar
- ☐ 1/2 c Boiling water
- ☐ Lemon gelatin (3 oz.)
- ☐ 1 qt Whipping cream

Directions:
Prepare your favorite graham cracker crust and press into the bottom and onto the sides of a 10" springform pan.

Bake or chill depending on your recipe's instructions.

Combine cream cheese, vanilla, and sugar. Beat until smooth and fluffy.

Bring water to a boil and add lemon gelatin. Stir until dissolved. Cool to room temperature and fold into cream cheese mixture.

Whip cream and fold into cream cheese mixture.

Pour into graham cracker crust and decorate with a few cracker crumbs.

Chill until firm and serve.

Simply Cheesecake

Amaretto Cheesecake

Ingredients:
- ☐ 6 Egg Beaters
- ☐ 1/2 c Sugar
- ☐ 1 ts Vanilla Extract
- ☐ 1 ts Almond Extract
- ☐ 2 tb Amaretto Liquor
- ☐ 2 lb Fat-Free Ricotta
- ☐ 6 tb Flour
- ☐ 1/2 ts Baking Powder
- ☐ Cinnamon as desired

Directions:
In a large bowl, combine egg substitute, sugar, vanilla, almond extract & amaretto. Beat with a wire whisk until frothy. Add ricotta & beat until smooth & creamy.

Combine flour & baking powder & add gradually to cheese mixture, blending thoroughly after each addition.

Pour into a 9" springform pan. Bake at 350 degree F for 1 hour or until toothpick inserted into center of cake comes out clean.

Cool; then remove springform rim & chill thoroughly in refrigerator.

Sprinkle with cinnamon before serving.

Simply Cheesecake

Autumn Cheesecake

Ingredients:
- ☐ 1 c Graham Cracker Crumbs
- ☐ 1/2 ts Cinnamon
- ☐ 16 oz Cream Cheese, Softened
- ☐ 2 Large Eggs
- ☐ 4 c Thinly Sliced Peeled Apples
- ☐ 1/2 ts Cinnamon
- ☐ 3 tb Sugar
- ☐ 1/4 c Margarine, Melted
- ☐ 1/2 c Sugar
- ☐ 1/2 ts Vanilla
- ☐ 1/3 c Sugar
- ☐ 1/4 c Chopped Pecans

Directions:
Combine crumbs, sugar, cinnamon and margarine, press onto bottom of 9-inch springform pan.

Bake at 350 degrees F., 10 minutes.

Combine cream cheese and sugar, mixing at medium speed on electric mixer, until well blended. Add eggs, one at a time, mixing well after each addition.

Blend in vanilla, pour over crust. Toss apples with combined sugar and cinnamon.

Spoon apple mixture over cream cheese layer; sprinkle with pecans.

Bake at 350 degrees F., 1 hour and 10 minutes.

Loosen cake from rim of pan; cool before removing rim of pan. Chill.

Aloha Cheesecake

Ingredients:
- ☐ 1 c Vanilla Wafer Crumbs
- ☐ 1/4 c Margarine, Melted
- ☐ 16 oz Cream Cheese, Softened
- ☐ 1/3 c Sugar
- ☐ 2 tb Milk
- ☐ 2 Large Eggs
- ☐ 1/2 c Macadamia Nuts, Toasted
- ☐ 8 1/2 oz Crushed Pineapple, Drained
- ☐ 1 Med Kiwi Peeled, Sliced

Directions:
Combine crumbs and margarine; press onto bottom of 9-inch springform pan.

Bake at 350 degrees F., 10 minutes.

Combine cream cheese, sugar and milk, mixing at medium speed on electric mixer until well blended.

Add eggs, one at a time, mixing well after each addition. Stir in nuts; pour over crust.

Bake at 350 degrees F., 45 minutes.

Loosen cake from rim of pan; cool before removing rim of pan. Chill. Before serving, top with fruit.

Simply Cheesecake

No Bake Lemon Cheesecake

Ingredients:
- ☐ 1 pk (3 oz.) lemon jello
- ☐ 1 c Boiling water
- ☐ 2 pk (8 oz.) cream cheese
- ☐ 1/2 c Sugar
- ☐ 1 ts Vanilla
- ☐ 1 Envelope Dream Whip instant topping mix

CRUST:
- ☐ 1 1/2 c Graham crumbs
- ☐ 1/3 c Sugar
- ☐ 6 tb Melted butter

Directions:
Combine graham cracker crumbs, sugar and butter; set aside 1/4 cup for topping.

Press remaining crumb mixture on bottom and sides and up to 1 1/2 inches in a 7x11x2-inch pan; set aside.

Dissolve lemon jello in small bowl with boiling water; chill until slightly thick.

Beat cream cheese, sugar and vanilla until fluffy. Beat in gelatin. Prepare whipped topping according to package directions.

Fold into cream cheese mixture. Pour into prepared pan; sprinkle with remaining crumbs.

Chill 3 to 4 hours before serving.

Simply Cheesecake

Banana Cheesecake

Ingredients:
- ☐ 1 10" pie crust, pre-baked for 10 minutes
- ☐ 12 oz Cream cheese
- ☐ 1 1/2 c Plain yogurt
- ☐ 2 c Pureed bananas (4 medium bananas)
- ☐ 2 Eggs (opt)
- ☐ 1/4 c Honey (optional)

Directions:
Blend all the ingredients in the blender until smooth and creamy.

Pour into the pre-baked pie crust and bake for 30 minutes at 350 or until set.

Allow to cool before serving.

You can top with a layer of yogurt and decorate with any fresh fruit (try a mixture of strawberry and banana slices). Serve well chilled.

Simply Cheesecake

Banana Nut Cheesecake

Ingredients:
- ☐ 1 c Chocolate wafer crumbs
- ☐ 1/4 c Margarine, melted
- ☐ 16 oz Cream cheese softened
- ☐ 1/2 c Sugar
- ☐ 1/2 c Mashed ripe bananas
- ☐ 2 lg Eggs
- ☐ 1/4 c Chopped walnuts
- ☐ 1/3 c Milk chocolate chips
- ☐ 1 tb Margarine
- ☐ 2 tb Water

Ingredients:
Combine crumbs and margarine; press onto the bottom of a 9-inch springform pan.

Bake at 350 degrees F., 10 minutes.

Combine cream cheese, sugar and banana, mixing at medium speed on electric mixer until well blended.

Add eggs, one at a time, mixing well after each addition. Stir in walnuts, pour over crust.

Bake at 350 degrees F., 40 minutes. Loosen cake from rim;cool before removing rim of pan.

Melt chocolate pieces and margarine with water over low heat, stirring until smooth. Drizzle over cheesecake. Chill.

Simply Cheesecake

Black Forest Cheesecake Delight

Ingredients:
- ☐ 1 c Chocolate Wafer Crumbs
- ☐ 3 tb Margarine, Melted
- ☐ 16 oz Cream Cheese Softened
- ☐ 2/3 c Sugar
- ☐ 2 Large Eggs
- ☐ 6 oz Semi-sweet Chocolate Chips, melted
- ☐ 1/4 ts Almond Extract
- ☐ 21 oz Cherry Pie Filling (1 Can)
- ☐ Frozen Whipped Topping Thawed

Directions:
Combine crumbs and margarine, press onto bottom of 9-inch springform pan.

Bake at 350 degrees F., 10 minutes.

Combine cream cheese and sugar, mixing at medium speed on electric mixer until well blended.

Add eggs, one at a time, mixing well after each addition. Blend in chocolate and extract; pour over crust.

Bake at 350 degrees F., 45 minutes. Loosen cake from rim of pan; cool before removing rim of pan. Chill.

Top cheesecake with pie filling and whipped topping just before serving.

Brownie Swirl Cheesecake

Ingredients:
- ☐ 8 oz (1 Pk) Brownie Mix
- ☐ 16 oz Cream Cheese, Softened
- ☐ 1/2 c Sugar
- ☐ 1 ts Vanilla
- ☐ 2 Large Eggs
- ☐ 1 c Milk Chocolate Chips, Melted

Directions:
Grease bottom of 9-inch Springform pan.

Prepare basic brownie mix as directed on package; pour batter evenly into springform pan.

Bake at 350 degrees F., 15 minutes.

Combine cream cheese, sugar and vanilla, mixing at medium speed on electric mixer until well blended. Add eggs, one at a time, mixing well after each addition. Pour over brownie layer.

Spoon chocolate over cream cheese mixture, cut through cheese and chocolate mixture several time to achieve a marble effect.

Bake at 350 degrees F., 35 minutes.

Loosen cake from rim of pan; cool before removing rim of pan. Chill.

Garnish with whipped cream, if desired.

Cranberry & White Chocolate Cheesecake

Ingredients:
Cake:
- ☐ 4 oz White chocolate, chopped
- ☐ 2 pk 8-oz cream cheese
- ☐ 3/4 c Sugar
- ☐ 3 Eggs
- ☐ 2 ts Vanilla
- ☐ pn Salt
- ☐ 3 c Sour cream

Crust:
- ☐ 1 c Graham cracker crumbs
- ☐ 2 tb Butter, melted
- ☐ 2 oz White chocolate, chopped

Glaze:
- ☐ 2 c Cranberries
- ☐ 1/3 c Sugar
- ☐ 1 ts Cornstarch
- ☐ Grated white chocolate for garnish if desired.

Directions:
Crust: Stir crumbs with butter until well moistened; stir in chocolate. Press into the bottom of a greased 9-inch springform pan.

Centre pan on a 20 X 14 inch piece of foil; press up tightly around side of pan.

Bake in 325F oven for 8 minutes. Let cool on a rack.

Cake: In a double boiler melt chocolate. Let cool. In a large bowl, beat cream cheese until softened.

Gradually beat in sugar; beat for 3 minutes or until fluffy. On low speed, beat in eggs, one at a time, beating well after each addition. Stir in vanilla, chocolate and salt; stir in sour cream. Pour onto crust.

Set cake pan onto a larger shallow pan; pour in enough hot water to come 1 inch up the side.

Bake at 325 degrees F for 1 1/4 hours or until the edge is set but centre still jiggles slightly. Turn oven off; let cool in oven for 1 hour.

Remove from larger pan and remove foil; let cool on a rack. Cover and refrigerate over night.

Glaze: In saucepan cook cranberries and 1/4 cup water, partially covered, just until boiling. Stir in sugar and return to a boil; cook for 2 minutes or until sugar is dissolved but berries have not popped. Drain, reserving juice and berries separately.

Remove cake from pan; place on cake plate.

Return juice to saucepan; blend in cornstarch.

Cook, whisking, until boiling and thickened; let cool slightly.

Spoon berries around edge of the cake. Spoon glaze over top.

Refrigerate for 1 hour or until set. Garnish with chocolate gratings.

Delectable Cheesecake

Ingredients:
Crust
- [ ] 1 1/2 c Graham cracker crumbs
- [ ] 2 tb Sugar
- [ ] 2/3 Cube margarine; melted

Filling
- [ ] 2 8 oz pkgs cream cheese; at room temperature
- [ ] 1/2 c Sugar
- [ ] 1/2 ts Vanilla
- [ ] 2 Eggs

Topping
- [ ] 1 c Sour cream
- [ ] 1/2 ts Vanilla
- [ ] 2 tb Sugar

Directions:
Stir together Crust Ingredients and press into 9 inch pie pan.

Bake at 350 for 5 minutes and set aside.

Beat Filling Ingredients well and pour into crust.

Bake at 350 for 20-30 minutes until not too jiggly in center.

Mix Topping Ingredients together and pour over top of cheese cake.

Bake at 350 for 5 minutes. Chill for 3 hours.

Top with your choice of pie filling, for example, cherry, lemon, raspberry or strawberry.

Serves 6-8.

Candy Cane Cheesecake

Ingredients:
- ☐ 1 1/3 c Chocolate Cookie Crumbs
- ☐ 2 tb Sugar
- ☐ 1/4 c Butter or margarine
- ☐ 1 1/2 c Sour Cream
- ☐ 1/2 c Sugar
- ☐ 3 Eggs
- ☐ 1 tb Flour
- ☐ 2 ts Vanilla
- ☐ 1/4 ts Peppermint extract
- ☐ 3 8oz packages of Cream Cheese
- ☐ 2 tb Butter
- ☐ 2/3 c Crushed peppermint candy

Directions:
Preheat oven to 325 degrees F.

Combine first 3 ingredients and press into a 9-inch springform pan.

Blend sour cream, sugar, eggs, flour and both extracts until smooth. Add cream cheese and 2 T butter. Stir in crushed candy.

Pour into crust and bake on lowest rack of oven for 50-60 minutes or until firm.

Allow to cool (top may crack) and refrigerate overnight.

Remove from pan and serve. Top with sweetened whip cream and garnish with candy cane if desired.

Simply Cheesecake

Black Forest Mini Cheesecakes

Ingredients:
- ☐ 24 Vanilla wafer cookies
- ☐ 16 oz Cream cheese; softened
- ☐ 1 1/4 c Sugar
- ☐ 1/3 c Hershey's Cocoa
- ☐ 2 tb All-purpose flour
- ☐ 3 Eggs
- ☐ 8 oz Dairy sour cream
- ☐ 1/2 ts Almond extract
- ☐ Canned cherry pie filling chilled

Sour Cream Topping
- ☐ 8 oz Dairy sour cream
- ☐ 2 tb Sugar
- ☐ 1 ts Vanilla extract

Directions:
Heat oven to 325 degrees F.

Line muffin cups (2-1/2 inches in diameter), with foil bake cups.

Place one vanilla wafer (flat-side down) in bottom of each cup.

In large bowl, beat cream cheese until smooth. Add sugar, cocoa and flour; blend well. Add eggs; beat well.

Stir in sour cream and almond extract. Fill each muffin cup almost full with batter.

Bake 20 to 25 minutes or until set.

Remove from oven; cool 5 to 10 minutes. Spread

heaping teaspoonful sour cream Topping on each cup.

Cool completely in pan on wire rack; refrigerate.

Just before serving, garnish with cherry pie filling. Cover; refrigerate leftover cheesecakes. 1-1/2 to 2 dozen cheesecakes.

Sour Cream Topping: In small bowl, stir together 1 container (8 oz.) dairy sour cream, 2 tablespoons sugar and 1 teaspoon vanilla extract; stir until sugar is dissolved.

Berry Good Cheesecake

Ingredients:
- ☐ 1 Envelope unflavored gelatin
- ☐ 1/4 c Orange juice
- ☐ 1/4 c Milk
- ☐ 1 Egg, separated
- ☐ 2/3 c 1% cottage cheese
- ☐ 2/3 c Yogurt cheese
- ☐ 7 tb Equal, sugar substitute
- ☐ Grated rind of 1 orange
- ☐ 1 Corn Flake Pie Crust
- ☐ 1 c Fresh strawberries, halved

Directions:
Smooth and so satisfying, no one will guess that this cheesecake is calorie and fat trim.

In 2 cup glass measure, sprinkle gelatin over orange juice.

Microwave at HIGH until gelatin dissolves. Stir in milk and egg yolk.

Microwave at medium for 30-60 seconds, or until hot and slightly thickened.

In food processor or blender, process cottage cheese until smooth; stir in yogurt cheese, 4 tbsp Equal, and orange rind.

With food processor or blender running, add gelatin mixture and process just until blended.

Refrigerate until consistency of egg whites. In separate bowl, beat egg white until soft peaks form.

Add 2 tbsp Equal and beat until stiff peaks form.

Fold into cheese mixture. Pour into corn flake pie crust and refrigerate several hours until set.

Just before serving, toss strawberry halves with remaining 1 tbsp Equal.

Arrange on cheesecake. Cut into 6 wedges.

Makes 6 servings.

Arkansas Cheesecake

Ingredients:
- ☐ 1 Egg, separated
- ☐ 1/2 c Skim milk
- ☐ 1 pk Gelatin (envelope)
- ☐ 1/8 ts Salt
- ☐ 1 tb Equal (no substitute)
- ☐ 1 1/2 c Cottage cheese
- ☐ 1 tb Lemon juice
- ☐ 1 ts Vanilla
- ☐ 6 tb Lite Cool whip

Directions:
Take cottage cheese and cream in blender until very SMOOTH. Set aside.

Put egg yolk in top of double boiler beat well and add milk. Add gelatin & salt.

Cook over boiling water until gelatin dissolves and mixture thickens. (about 10 minutes) Remove from heat, add sugar substitute.

Cool. Add cottage cheese, lemon juice and vanilla to cooled mixture.

Chill, stirring occasionally, until mixture mounds when dropped from a spoon. Beat egg white until stiff.

Fold egg white and cool whip together into mixture. Pour into graham crust. Or pour into pie plate and top with crumb topping.

Crumb Topping: crush 2 graham crackers fine.

Mix with pinch of cinnamon and nutmeg.

Cheesecake Banana

Ingredients:
Crust:
- [ ] 1 1/2 c Graham Cracker Crumbs
- [ ] 1/4 c Sugar; Granulated

Cheesecake:
- [ ] 1 lb Cream Cheese
- [ ] 1/4 c Sugar; Granulated
- [ ] 2 ts Lemon Juice
- [ ] 4 Eggs; Large
- [ ] 1 c Sour Cream
- [ ] 1 c Bananas; Mashed; *
- [ ] 6 tb Butter; Melted

Directions:
* Approximately 3 medium bananas should yield the 1 cup of mashed.

Crust: Preheat the oven to 350 degrees F.

Place the crumbs in a mixing bowl and add the butter and sugar. Blend well.

Press the crumb mixture onto the bottom and partly up the sides of a greased 9-inch springform pan.

Smooth the crumb mixture along the bottom to an even thickness.

Bake for about 10 minutes in the oven at 350 degrees F. Cool before filling.

Cheesecake: Preheat the oven to 350 degrees F.

Simply Cheesecake

In a large mixing bowl; beat the cream cheese, sugar and lemon juice together. Add the eggs, one at a time, beating well after each addition.
Stir in the sour cream and the mashed bananas and blend well until very smooth.

Pour the mixture into the prepared crust and bake for 1 hour.

Cool in the oven, with the door propped open, until the cake is at room temperature.

Chill until serving time.

Cheesecake Pecan Pie

Ingredients:
- ☐ 8 oz Cream cheese, softened
- ☐ 1 Egg
- ☐ 1/3 c Sugar
- ☐ 1 ts Vanilla
- ☐ 1 Unbaked 9 inch pie shell
- ☐ 1 1/2 c Pecan halves
- ☐ 2 Slightly beaten eggs
- ☐ 1/4 c Sugar
- ☐ 2/3 c Light corn syrup
- ☐ 1/2 ts Vanilla

Directions:
Combine cream cheese, egg, 1/3 cup sugar, and 1 teaspoon vanilla. Beat until light and fluffy.

Spread over bottom of pie shell. Arrange pecans on the cream cheese mixture.

Mix remaining eggs, sugar, corn syrup, and vanilla, stirring well.

Carefully pour over the pecans.

Bake at 375 degrees for 40 to 45 minutes or until done.

Simply Cheesecake

Cappuccino Chocolate Cheesecake

Ingredients:
- ☐ 1 1/4 c Chocolate wafers, crushed
- ☐ 1/8 ts Cinnamon
- ☐ 1 pk Light cream cheese (8 oz)
- ☐ 1 c Sugar
- ☐ 1 c Unsweetened cocoa powder
- ☐ 1 ts Cocoa powder for garnish
- ☐ 2 1/2 c Sour cream
- ☐ 2 Eggs
- ☐ 2 tb Coffee liqueur
- ☐ 1 ts Vanilla

Directions:
Preheat oven to 350 degrees F.

Stir together wafer crumbs and cinnamon. Pat into bottom of 9- inch springform pan.

Beat cream cheese until light and fluffy. Beat in sugar and cocoa powder. Beat in egg.

Stir in 2 cups sour cream, coffee liqueur and vanilla.

Turn into prepared pan. Bake for 30 minutes or until set.

Spread remaining sour cream evenly over top.

Return to oven 1 minute to glaze top.

Cool to room temperature, then chill thoroughly, covered.

Simply Cheesecake

Remove from springform pan. Just before serving, dust top with cocoa powder.

Cheesecake with Raspberry Sauce

Ingredients:
- ☐ 1/4 c Graham Cracker Crumbs
- ☐ 500 ml Cottage Cheese, 2% Fat
- ☐ 500 g Cream Cheese - Fat Free Philadelphia
- ☐ 1 c Sugar
- ☐ 2 tb Cornstarch
- ☐ 1 ts Vanilla Extract
- ☐ 1 ea Egg
- ☐ 2 ea Egg Whites
- ☐ 300 g Raspberries, Frozen Thawed
- ☐ 1 tb Cornstarch
- ☐ 1/2 c Jelly

Directions:
Sprinkle graham crumbs evenly over bottom of lightly greased 9 inch springform pan.

Puree well drained cottage cheese in processor until smooth. Add cream cheese, cut into cubes and continue processing until smooth.

With processor on, gradually add sugar, cornstarch and vanilla. Add egg and egg whites, one at a time to cream cheese mixture; process using on and off action until just blended; pour into pan.

Bake at 450 for 10 min.; reduce to 250 and bake 35 - 40 min. Cool.

Refrigerate overnight. Serve with Raspberry sauce.

Raspberry Sauce: Drain thawed, frozen raspberries, reserving juice. Place berries in sieve;

crush to extract additional juice.

Discard seeds. Whisk cornstarch and heated jelly into juice.

Cook sauce in microwave on High until thickened (1-2 min).

Refrigerate until cool.

Makes 1 1/4 cups.

Apple Cheesecake

Ingredients:
- ☐ 1 c Graham cracker crumbs
- ☐ Sugar
- ☐ 1 ts Cinnamon; divided
- ☐ 3 tb Margarine; melted
- ☐ 16 oz Cream cheese; softened
- ☐ 2 Eggs
- ☐ 1/2 ts Vanilla extract
- ☐ 4 c Apple slices; thinly sliced, peeled, about 2 1/2 lbs apples
- ☐ 1/2 c Pecans; chopped

Directions:
Preheat oven to 350 degrees F.

Combine crumbs, 3 tablespoons sugar, 1/2 teaspoon cinnamon and margarine in small bowl; mix well.

Press onto bottom and up sides of 9-inch pie plate. Bake crust 10 minutes.

Beat together cream cheese and 1/2 cup sugar in large bowl until well blended. Add eggs, one at a time, beating well after each addition.

Blend in vanilla; pour into crust. Combine remaining 1/3 cup sugar and remaining 1/2 teaspoon cinnamon in large bowl.

Add apples; toss gently to coat. Spoon apple mixture over cream cheese mixture.

Sprinkle with pecans. : Bake 1 hour and 10

minutes or until set. Loosen cake from rim of pan; cool before removing rim of pan. Refrigerate.

Amaretto Cheesecake

Ingredients:
- ☐ 1 1/2 c graham cracker crushed
- ☐ 1/2 Stick butter, melted
- ☐ 15 oz Ricotta cheese
- ☐ 8 oz Cream cheese
- ☐ 4 Eggs, lightly beaten
- ☐ 1/2 c Sugar
- ☐ 1/3 c Amaretto liquor
- ☐ 1 ts Vanilla
- ☐ 1/4 ts Salt

Directions:
Combine crumbs of graham crackers and butter; press over bottom and sides of greased 9 inch spring- form pan. Chill.

Preheat oven to 325.

Beat together ricotta and cream cheese until smooth.

Pour mixture into pan; bake 1 hour and 15 minutes, or until firm in middle.

Cool 30 minutes in pan before removing. Cool completely (preferably in refrigerator overnight) before serving.

Top with fresh fruit, or jam.

Great topped with strawberry jam.

Simply Cheesecake

Amaretto Hazelnut Macaroon Cheesecake

Ingredients:
Hazelnut Crust
- ☐ 1 c Hazelnuts, roast 10 min at 350
- ☐ 3 Egg whites
- ☐ 2 ts Vanilla
- ☐ 2 c Powdered sugar
- ☐ 1/2 c Sugar
- ☐ 1/8 ts Salt

Filling:
- ☐ 1/2 c Amaretto
- ☐ 3 ts Gelatin, unflavored
- ☐ 2 ts Vanilla
- ☐ 1 1/2 lb Cream cheese
- ☐ 3/4 c Sugar
- ☐ 2 tb Lemon juice
- ☐ 1 ts Lemon zest
- ☐ 2 c Cream

Directions:
Hazelnut macaroon: heat oven to 350.

Grease 10 inch springform pan. Line with parchment. Grease parchment. Line a cookie sheet with greased parchment.

Whisk together eggs and vanilla. Remove as much skin from the hazelnuts as is convenient.

Chop the nuts in a food processor with one cup of the powdered sugar for 30 sec.

Add both powdered and regular sugar. Pulse a few

times to combine.

With processor running, pour in egg mixture.
process for 15 sec until smooth
Reserve and set aside 1/2 - 1/3 cup batter.

Pour remaining into springform, smooth with
spatula.

Pour reserved batter onto cookie sheet, spread in a
7-8 inch disk.

Bake crust 25-30 min., disk 20-25 min. cool on
wire rack

Chop up the disk into 1/8 inch pieces and soak in
1/4 amaretto.

Carefully remove crust. Replace bottom of
springform with foil wrapped cardboard circle.
Replace crust.

Amaretto cheesecake filling: sprinkle gelatin
over 1/4 cp amaretto, let stand 5 min.

Heat in sauce pan with hot (not boiling) water
stirring for 4 min., leave in hot water to stay warm

Beat cream cheese in mixer for 1 min. Add lemon
juice and zest, mix. Beat cream to soft peaks.

Fold 1/3 cream into cream cheese. Fold in
remaining whipped cream.

Fold in soaked macaroon disk bits Scrape into
prepared pan, cover with plastic wrap.

Refrigerate at least 3 hrs. (preferably overnight)

Simply Cheesecake

Amaretto Chocolate Cheesecake

Ingredients:
Crust
- [ ] 7 oz Amaretti (see note)
- [ ] 1 oz Chocolate, unsweetened, 1 square
- [ ] 2 tb Granulated sugar
- [ ] 5 tb Sweet butter

Filling:
- [ ] 6 oz Chocolate, semisweet
- [ ] 1 1/2 lb Cream cheese
- [ ] 7 oz Amaretti
- [ ] 4 oz Almond paste
- [ ] 4 lg Eggs
- [ ] 1/3 c Amaretto liqueur
- [ ] 1/2 c Heavy cream
- [ ] 1/4 c Sugar, granulated

Directions:
Crust: Butter the sides only (not the bottom) of a 9-inch spring-form pan (about 2 1/2 to 3 inches deep).

Grind the Amaretti very fine in a food processor or blender. Mix with sugar in a mixing bowl.

Melt the chocolate and butter in the top of a double boiler, stirring occasionally.

Add the melted mixture to the Amaretti crumbs and sugar and mix thoroughly. (Don't wash the double boiler; you'll be using it again in a minute.)

Turn the mixture into the prepared pan. With your fingers, distribute it evenly over the bottom and press it down into a very firm, compact layer.

Refrigerate while you prepare the filling.

Make Filling: Adjust rack 1/3 up from the bottom of the oven and preheat to 350 degrees F.

Partially melt chocolate in the top of a double boiler, then uncover and stir until completely melted.

Remove the top of the double boiler and set aside to cool.

Break the Amaretti coarsely into a bowl and set aside.

Cut the almond paste into small pieces, and beat on low speed with an electric mixer, while gradually adding the Amaretto liqueur. Beat until thoroughly mixed and set aside.

Beat the cream cheese with an electric mixer until smooth. Add the sugar and beat until smooth again.

Add the almond paste- Amaretto mixture and beat until thoroughly mixed. Add the melted chocolate and beat well again.

Add the eggs one at a time, beating at low speed until they are incorporated after each addition.

Add the heavy cream and beat until smooth. Add the coarsely broken Amaretti and stir gently only to mix.

Turn into the prepared pan, pouring the mixture over the bottom crust. Rotate the pan gently to level the batter. (Don't worry if the mixture comes almost to the top; it won't run over.)

Bake 45 minutes. It will seem soft and not done, but don't bake any more; it will become firm when chilled.

The top of the cake is supposed to look bumpy because of the large chunks of Amaretti.

Let cool completely at room temperature, then carefully remove the sides of the pan and refrigerate the cake (still on the bottom of the pan) for 4 to 6 hours, or overnight.

Amaretto Cheesecake with Raspberry Sauce

Ingredients:
Base:
- ☐ 1/4 c Butter
- ☐ 2 c Almonds, chopped
- ☐ 2 tb Granulated sugar

Filling:
- ☐ 12 oz Cream cheese, softened
- ☐ 1/2 c Granulated sugar
- ☐ 3 Eggs
- ☐ 1 c Sour cream
- ☐ 2 tb Amaretto
- ☐ 1/2 ts Vanilla
- ☐ 1/2 ts Almond extract

Sauce:
- ☐ 3 c Raspberries, frozen, unsweetened, thawed
- ☐ 2 tb Amaretto
- ☐ Sugar

Directions:
Base: In 9-inch microwavable quiche dish, shallow round baking dish or deep pie plate, melt butter at high (100 per cent power) 1 to 1 1/2 minutes.

Stir in almonds and sugar until evenly coated with butter.

Press into bottom and sides of dish. Microwave at high 2 to 3 minutes or until firm. If necessary, rotate dish during cooking.

Filling: Beat cream cheese and sugar until light. Beat in eggs one at a time. Add sour cream, 2 tablespoons Amaretto or almond liqueur, vanilla and almond extract. Beat until smooth.

Pour into baked crust. Microwave uncovered at medium (50 per cent power) 14 to 18 minutes or until cheesecake is almost set in centre.

Rotate dish partway through cooking, if necessary. Cool on countertop to room temperature, then cover and refrigerate until serving time.

Sauce: Reserve some whole raspberries for garnish. Puree remaining raspberries. Push through sieve to remove seeds.

Stir 2 tablespoons Amaretto or almond liqueur into puree. Add sugar to taste.

To serve, spoon some sauce on to dessert plates. Place slice of cheesecake on sauce. Garnish with reserved berries.

Makes 6 to 8 servings.

If you prefer, use 1 cup graham cracker crumbs with 1/2 cup finely chopped almonds for the crust.

Use a food processor and pulse to chop nuts to an even consistency, rather than a fine powder.

Also, you could substitute strawberries for the raspberries.

To omit liqueur, increase almond extract in the filling to 1 teaspoon and use just a drop in the raspberry puree.

Simply Cheesecake

Amaretto Cheesecake Extraordinaire

Ingredients:
Crust:
- ☐ 1 1/2 c Graham cracker crumbs
- ☐ 2 tb Sugar
- ☐ 1 ts Cinnamon
- ☐ 1 Stick margarine; melted

Cake:
- ☐ 24 oz Cream cheese
- ☐ 1 c Sugar
- ☐ 4 Eggs
- ☐ 1/3 c Amaretto (up to 1/2 cup)

Topping:
- ☐ 8 oz Sour cream
- ☐ 1 tb Plus 1 tsp. sugar
- ☐ 1 tb Amaretto

Garnishes:
- ☐ Almond halves
- ☐ Shavings from a Hershey bar

Directions:
Combine crust ingredients and press into the bottom and sides of a 10" springform pan.

Combine cake ingredients and pour into the crust.

Bake at 375 F. for 45 to 50 minutes.

Turn the oven to 500 degrees F.

Meanwhile, combine topping ingredients. Spread on the cheesecake and return to the oven for five minutes.

Chill overnight and garnish as desired.

Simply Cheesecake

Amaretto Cheesecake Delight

Ingredients:
- ☐ 3 pk Cream cheese -- 8oz.
- ☐ 1 c Sugar
- ☐ 4 lg Eggs
- ☐ 1/3 c Amaretto
- ☐ 1 1/2 c Graham cracker crumbs
- ☐ 1 ts Cinnamon
- ☐ 1/4 c Sugar
- ☐ 6 tb Butter -- Melted
- ☐ 8 oz Sour Cream
- ☐ 1 tb Sugar (plus 1 teaspoon)
- ☐ 1 tb Amaretto

Directions:
Mix graham cracker crumbs, cinnamon, sugar and butter.

Pat mixture in bottom of a 9 inch springform pan.

Beat cram cheese until light and fluffy. Gradually beat in 1 cup sugar. Add eggs one at a time beating well after each addition.

Pour into and and bake in a pre-heated 375 degree F oven for 45-50 minutes.

Mix the sour cream, sugar and amaretto.

Spoon the mixture over the cheesecake when done and return to oven for 5 minutes at 500'.

Let ripen 48 hours in the refrigerator.

Top with 1/4 cup sliced toasted almonds, and

chocolate curls before serving.

Serving Ideas : Top with sliced, toasted almonds and chocolate curls.

Gala Apricot Cheesecake

Ingredients:
- ☐ 2 1/4 c Quick Oats, Uncooked
- ☐ 1/3 c Brown Sugar, Packed
- ☐ 3 tb Unbleached All-purpose Flour
- ☐ 1/3 c Margarine, Melted
- ☐ 1 ea Env. Unflavored Gelatin
- ☐ 1/3 c Cold Water
- ☐ 16 oz Cream Cheese, Softened
- ☐ 1/2 c Granulated Sugar
- ☐ 2 tb Brandy
- ☐ 1/2 c Dried Apricots, Fine Chop
- ☐ 1 c Whipping Cream, Whipped
- ☐ 10 oz (1 Jr) Apricot Preserves
- ☐ 1 tb Brandy

Directions:
Combine oats, brown sugar, flour and margarine, press onto bottom of 9-inch springform pan.

Bake at 350 degrees F., 15 minutes. Cool.

Soften gelatin in water; stir over low heat until dissolved.

Combine Cream Cheese and granulated sugar, mixing at medium speed on electric mixer until well blended. Gradually add gelatin and brandy to cream cheese mixture mixing until well blended.

Chill until slightly thickened; fold in apricots and whipped cream. Pour into crust; chill until firm.

Heat combined preserves and brandy over low heat; cool. Spoon over cheesecake.

VARIATION: Substitute Neufchatel cheese for Cream Cheese.

Amaretto Cheesecake with Apricot Glaze

Ingredients:
Crust:
- [ ] 1 c Graham Wafer Crumbs
- [ ] 1/2 c Almonds, chopped toasted, unblanched
- [ ] 2 tb Sugar
- [ ] 1/4 c Butter, melted

Filling:
- [ ] 4 pk Cream Cheese(250g), softened
- [ ] 1 c Sugar
- [ ] 3 tb Flour
- [ ] 4 ea Eggs
- [ ] 1 c Sour Cream
- [ ] 1/4 c Amaretto liqueur

Glaze:
- [ ] 1/2 c Apricot Jam
- [ ] 1 tb Amaretto liqueur

Directions:
Crust: Combine ingredients; press onto bottom of a 9-inch springform pan. Set aside.

Filling: Combine cream cheese, sugar, and flour, mixing until well blended. Add eggs, one at a time, mixing just until combined.

Blend in sour cream and liqueur; pour over crust.

Bake in 450 degree F oven 10 minutes. Reduce oven temperature to 250 degrees F; continue baking for 1 hour.

Run knife around rim of pan; cool on wire rack. Chill.

Glaze: To glaze cake, combine jam and liqueur in a saucepan; heat until warm and smooth.

Strain mixture and pour over cheesecake before removing sides of pan.

Garnish if desired.

Makes 10-12 servings.

Simply Cheesecake

Amaretto Mousse Cheesecake

Ingredients:
- ☐ 2 c Graham cracker crumbs
- ☐ 1/2 c Butter or margarine, melted
- ☐ 1 Envelope unflavored Gelatin
- ☐ 1/2 c Cold Water*
- ☐ 3 pk (8 oz each) cream cheese, softened
- ☐ 1 1/4 c Sugar
- ☐ 1 cn (5 oz) evaporated milk
- ☐ 1 ts Lemon juice
- ☐ 1/3 c Amaretto liqueur
- ☐ 1 ts Vanilla extract
- ☐ 3/4 c Whipping or heavy cream, whipped

Directions:
Combine graham cracker crumbs with butter. Press onto bottom and up sides of 9-inch springform pan; chill.

In small saucepan sprinkle gelatin over cold water. Let stand 1 minute. Stir over low heat till completely dissolved, about 3 minutes; set aside.

In large bowl of electric mixer, beat cream cheese with sugar till fluffy, about 2 minutes. Gradually add evaporated milk and lemon; beat at medium-high speed till mixture is very fluffy, about 2 minutes.

Gradually beat in gelatin mixture, liqueur and vanilla thoroughly blended. Fold in whipped cream.

Pour into crust; chill 8 hours or overnight.

Simply Cheesecake

Garnish with chocolate sauce and berries.

*Substitution: Omit amaretto liqueur. Increase water to 3/4 cup, add 1/2 teaspoon almond extract with vanilla.

Gradually add evaporated milk and lemon juice; beat at medium-high speed till mixture is very fluffy, about 2 minute.

Gradually beat in gelatin mixture, liqueur and vanilla until thoroughly blended.

Fold in whipped cream. Pour into crust; chill 8 hours or overnight.

Garnish with chocolate sauce and berries.

Cheesecake Cupcakes

Ingredients:
- ☐ 3 pk 8 oz Cream Cheese
- ☐ 1 c Sugar
- ☐ 1 tb Vanilla
- ☐ 3 Eggs
- ☐ 1 c Sour cream
- ☐ Custard Cups

Directions:
Leave cream cheese out to soften.

Beat until smooth with sugar and vanilla. Add eggs, one at a time, beating on high.

Fold in sour cream.

Will make more than what a 9" graham cracker crust will hold, so fill it to the brim, and then bake the remainder in custard cup(s).

Bake at 350F for 30-35 minutes, or until crust is golden brown and toothpick comes out clean.

Simply Cheesecake

Chocolate Cheesecake

Ingredients:
- ☐ 1/2 8 1/2-oz package chocolate wafers
- ☐ 1 tb Butter, softened
- ☐ 4 8-oz packages cream cheese, softened
- ☐ 1/2 c Sugar
- ☐ 2 tb Cornstarch
- ☐ 4 lg Eggs
- ☐ 1 tb Vanilla
- ☐ 3 1-oz squares semisweet chocolate, melted & cooled
- ☐ 1 8-oz container sour cream

Directions:
Heat oven to 300 degrees F.

Crush chocolate wafers in food processor or in plastic bag with rolling pin. Add butter and process or knead into crumbs.

Pat into bottom of an oiled 9-inch spring-form pan. Bake 10 minutes.

In the large bowl of an electric mixer, beat cream cheese until fluffy. Stir together sugar and cornstarch.

Beat into cream cheese mixture. Add eggs to mixture one at a time, beating after each addition. Fold in vanilla, chocolate, and sour cream until uniformly combined.

Turn cheesecake mixture into hot, crumb-lined pan.

Carefully return to oven. Bake until center of cake seems to be almost set when the pan is gently tapped-about 1 hour.

Turn off oven and allow cake to sit in oven 1 hour longer.

Remove pan from oven; cool to room temperature. Cover without touching surface of cake.

Place in refrigerator overnight.

To serve, loosen cake from side of pan with a spatula. Remove side of pan.

Place cake on serving platter.

Decorate with whipped cream, if desired.

Very Blueberry Cheesecake

Ingredients:
- ☐ 1 1/2 c Vanilla Wafer Crumbs
- ☐ 1/4 c Margarine, Melted
- ☐ 1 ea Env. Unflavored Gelatin
- ☐ 1/4 c Cold Water
- ☐ 16 oz Cream Cheese, Softened
- ☐ 1 tb Lemon Juice
- ☐ 1 ts Grated Lemon Peel
- ☐ 7 oz (1 jr) Marshmallow Crème
- ☐ 3 c Frozen Whipped Topping(thaw)
- ☐ 2 c Blueberries Frozen or Fresh

Directions:
Combine crumbs and margarine, press onto bottom of 9-inch springform pan. Chill.

Soften gelatin in water, stir over low heat until dissolved. Gradually add gelatin to cream cheese, mixing at medium speed on electric mixer until well blended.

Blend in juice and peel. Beat in marshmallow crème; fold in whipped topping.

Puree blueberries; fold into cream cheese mixture. Chill until firm.

Garnish with additional frozen whipped topping, thawed, and lemon peel.

Very Smooth Cheesecake

Ingredients:
- ☐ 1 c Graham Cracker Crumbs
- ☐ 3 tb Sugar
- ☐ 3 tb Margarine, Melted
- ☐ 1 ea Env Unflavored Gelatin
- ☐ 1/4 c Cold Water
- ☐ 8 oz Cream Cheese, Softened
- ☐ 1/2 c Sugar
- ☐ 10 oz Frozen Strawberries, Thawed
- ☐ 1 x Milk
- ☐ 1 c Whipping Cream, Whipped

Directions:
Combine crumbs and margarine; press onto bottom of 9-inch springform pan.

Bake at 325 degreees F., 10 minutes. Cool.

Soften gelatin in water; stir over low heat until dissolved.

Combine cream cheese and sugar, mixing at medium speed on electric mixer until well blended.

Drain strawberries, reserving liquid. Add enough milk to liquid to measure 1 cup. Gradually add combined milk mixture and gelatin to cream cheese, mixing until well blended.

Chill until slightly thickened.

Fold in whipped cream and strawberries; pour over crust. Chill until firm.

Chocolate Cheesecake

Ingredients:
- ☐ 8 1/2 oz Chocolate Wafers, Fine Crush
- ☐ 1/2 c Butter, Melted
- ☐ 12 oz Semi-sweet Chocolate Chips
- ☐ 1 1/2 c Heavy cream
- ☐ 16 oz Cream Cheese, Softened
- ☐ 1/4 c Sugar
- ☐ 4 ea Large Eggs
- ☐ 1 ts Vanilla Extract
- ☐ 1/2 c Heavy Cream Whipped (Opt.)

Directions:
In large bowl, combine chocolate wafer crumbs and butter. Pat fimly into 9-inch springform pan, covering bottom and 2 1/2 inches up sides. Chill.

Preheat oven to 325 degrees F.

Combine over hot (not boiling) water, chocolate chips and heavy cream. Stir until morsels are melted and mixture is smooth. Set aside.

In large bowl, combine cream cheese and sugar, beating untl creamy. Add eggs, one at a time, beating well after each addition. Add chocolate mixture and vanilla, mix until blended. Pour into prepared crust.

Bake at 325 degrees F. for 60 minutes. Turn oven off. Let stand in oven with door ajar 1 hour.

Remove, cool completely. Chill 24 hours.

Decorate edge with whipped cream, if desired.

Simply Cheesecake

Chocolate Caramel Pecan Cheesecake

Ingredients:
Base:
- ☐ 2 c Vanilla wafer crumbs
- ☐ 6 tb Margarine, melted

Body:
- ☐ 1 ea 14-ounce bag caramels
- ☐ 1 cn 5-ounce evaporated milk
- ☐ 1 c Chopped pecans, toasted
- ☐ 2 pk 8-ounce cream cheese, soften
- ☐ 1/2 c Sugar
- ☐ 1 ts Vanilla
- ☐ 2 ea Eggs
- ☐ 1/2 c Semi-sweet chocolate pieces

Directions:
Base: Combine crumbs and margarine; press onto bottom of 9-inch springform pan.

Bake at 350 degree F, 10 minutes.

Body In 1 1/2 quart heavy saucepan, melt caramels with milk over low heat, stirring frequently, until smooth. Pour over crust. Top with pecans.

Combine cream cheese, sugar and vanilla, mixing at medium speed on electric mixer until well blended. Add eggs, one at a time, mixing well after each addition. Blend in chocolate; pour over pecans.

Bake at 350 degrees F, 40 minutes.

Loosen cake from rim of pan; cool before removing

rim of pan. Chill. Garnish with whipped cream
and additional finely chopped pecans, if desired.

Aunt Franny's Cheesecake

Ingredients:
- ☐ 3 pk Cream cheese
- ☐ 5 Eggs
- ☐ 1 1/2 pt Sour cream
- ☐ 1 1/2 ts Vanilla
- ☐ 3 tb Sugar
- ☐ 1 c Granulated sugar
- ☐ 1 1/2 ts Vanilla
- ☐ 1/2 c Sugar
- ☐ 1 1/2 c Graham cracker crumbs
- ☐ 1/4 c Margarine

Crust:
- ☐ 1 1/2 c. graham cracker crumbs
- ☐ 3 T. sugar
- ☐ 1/4 cup margarine.

Directions:
Crust: Mix and pour in 13x9x2 pan. Pat to edges, filling pan

Filling: Cream cheese, add eggs, one at a time; mix thoroughly. Add 1 cup sugar and 1 1/2 t. vanilla.

Pour over graham cracker crust. Bake at 300 for one hour. Cool for 5 minutes.

Topping: Mix 1 1/2 pts. sour cream, 1/2 c sugar, and 1 1/2 t. vanilla together. Pour over baked cheesecake.

Bake an additional 5 minutes in oven, set overnight. Serve cherry pie filling as topping on the side. Cherries might be too rich for some people so this enables anyone who wants them to add them individually.

Chocolate Cheesecake Delight

Ingredients:
- ☐ 16 oz Vanilla low fat yogurt
- ☐ 30 oz Part-skim ricotta cheese
- ☐ 1/2 c Chocolate wafer crumbs (about 10 wafers)
- ☐ 2 Egg whites
- ☐ 3/4 c Sugar
- ☐ 1/2 c Cocoa powder
- ☐ 2 tb Flour
- ☐ 2 ts Vanilla
- ☐ Non dairy whipped topping
- ☐ Strawberry halves

Directions:
Line two colanders with paper toweling. Place yogurt in one and ricotta cheese in the other. Place in refrigerator for 24 hours.

Preheat oven to 325 deg f.

Sprinkle crumbs on bottom of a 9" springform pan.

In the bowl of a food processor - puree the ricotta cheese until very smooth (about 6-8 minutes, until cheese feels smooth when rubbed between your fingertips).

Add drained yogurt, egg whites, sugar, cocoa, flour and vanilla. Puree for 3 minutes. Spoon the cheese mixture over the crumbs.

Bake for 50 minutes or until edges are set. Turn off oven; open door slightly. Leave cheese cake in oven for 1 hour or overnight until cold.

Garnish. Makes 16 servings.

Holiday Delight Cheesecake

Ingredients:
- ☐ 1 c Graham cracker crumbs
- ☐ 3 tb Sugar
- ☐ 2 tb Margarine, melted
- ☐ 3 pk Fat-free Cream Cheese (8oz)
- ☐ 3/4 c Sugar
- ☐ 2 tb Flour
- ☐ 3 tb Lemon juice
- ☐ 3 tb Cholesterol-free egg product
- ☐ 1 ct Non-fat lemon yogurt
- ☐ Lite whipped topping
- ☐ 1 cn Cherry pie filling

Directions:
Heat oven to 350 degrees F.

Combine graham cracker crumbs, sugar and margarine; mix well. Pat onto bottom of 9" or 10" springform pan. Set aside.

Beat cream cheese, sugar and flour together until light, fluffy and smooth. Gradually add lemon juice and egg product; beat well. Add lemon yogurt and mix thoroughly. Pour over prepared crust.

Loosely place aluminum foil over springform pan.

Bake at 350 degrees F 60 to 70 minutes or until center of cake is set.

Gently run tip of knife between cake and edge of pan. Cool to room temperature before removing from pan. Chill.

Served topped with cherry pie filling and whipped topping.

Cheddar Chili Cheesecake

Ingredients:
- ☐ 1 1/2 tb Butter -- (for pan)
- ☐ 1/4 c Breadcrumbs -- fine, toasted
- ☐ 1/4 c Cheddar cheese -- finely grated
- ☐ 6 oz Ham -- thinly sliced
- ☐ 1 1/2 lb Cream cheese -- room temperature
- ☐ 3/4 lb Cheddar cheese -- grated, sharp
- ☐ 1 c Cottage cheese
- ☐ 3/4 c Chopped green onions
- ☐ 4 Eggs
- ☐ 3 tb Jalapeno pepper -- optional
- ☐ 2 tb Milk
- ☐ 1 Clove garlic -- halved

Directions:
Preheat oven to 325 degrees F.
Butter 9" springform pan. Mix breadcrumbs and 1/4 cup cheddar. Sprinkle mixture into pan, turning to coat. Refrigerate.

Dice about half of ham; reserve remaining slices. Mix diced ham with remaining ingredients in blender or processor until smooth.

Pour slightly more than half of filling into prepared pan. Top with reserved ham slices in even layer. Cover with remaining filling.

Set pan on baking sheet. Bake 1 1/4 hours. Turn oven off and cool cheesecake about 1 hour with door ajar.

Transfer cheesecake to rack. Remove sides of pan. Cool to room temperature before serving.

Simply Cheesecake

Auntie Babe's Cheesecake

Ingredients:
Crust:
- ☐ 1 2/3 c Graham cracker crumbs
- ☐ 1 1/2 ts Cinnamon
- ☐ 2 tb Sugar
- ☐ 6 tb Butter; melted

Filling:
- ☐ 1 c Sugar
- ☐ 3 Eggs; beaten well
- ☐ 24 oz Cream cheese; softened
- ☐ 1/2 ts Vanilla

Topping:
- ☐ 1 pt Sour cream
- ☐ 3 tb Sugar
- ☐ 1/2 ts Vanilla

Directions:
Combine crust ingredients and pat into bottom and sides of pan.

Beat cream cheese thoroughly; add sugar gradually; add eggs in thirds; add vanilla; pour into prepared pan.

Bake at 375 degrees F. for 25 minutes; remove from oven and add topping.

To prepare topping, whip sour cream; add sugar and vanilla, and pour over cake.

Continue baking at 500 for 5 minutes.

Important - chill at LEAST 24 hours.

Holiday Eggnog Cheesecake

Ingredients:
- ☐ 1 c Graham cracker crumbs
- ☐ 1/4 t Ground nutmeg
- ☐ 1 ea Env. unflavored gelatin
- ☐ 8 oz Cream cheese, softened
- ☐ 1 c Eggnog
- ☐ 1/4 c Sugar
- ☐ 1/4 c Margarine, melted
- ☐ 1/4 c Cold water
- ☐ 1/4 c Sugar
- ☐ 1 c Whipping cream, whipped

Directions:
Combine crumbs, sugar, nutmeg and margarine; press onto bottom of 9-inch springform pan.

Soften gelatin in water; stir over low heat until dissolved. Combine cream cheese and sugar, at medium speed on electric mixer until well blended.

Gradually add gelatin and eggnog, mixing until blended. Chill until slightly thickened; fold in whipped cream.

Pour over crust; chill until firm.

VARIATION: Increase sugar to 1/3 c. Substitute milk for eggnog. Add 1 t vanilla and 3/4 t rum extract.

Cheddar Cheesecake with Strawberries

Ingredients:
- ☐ 1 1/4 c Vanilla wafer crumbs
- ☐ 2 tb Butter or margarine -- Melted
- ☐ 16 oz Cream cheese -- softened
- ☐ 1/2 c Shredded sharp cheddar cheese
- ☐ 3/4 c Sugar
- ☐ 3 Eggs
- ☐ 1/2 ts Grated orange peel
- ☐ 1/4 ts Grated lemon peel
- ☐ 2 tb Flour
- ☐ 1 c Heavy cream
- ☐ 1 pt Fresh strawberries
- ☐ Light corn syrup

Directions:

Mix crumbs with butter; press over bottom of nine-inch springform pan.

Bake in 350 degree F oven for 5 minutes.

Combine cheeses and sugar in bowl; beat until fluffy. Beat in eggs, one at a time. Blend in peels, flour, and 1/2 cup of the cream.

Pour over crumb crust in pan.

Bake at 350 for 40 minutes or until cake is set in center. Cool on rack.

Arrange the whole strawberries on top of the cake. Brush with corn syrup.

Simply Cheesecake

Absolutely Delicious Cheesecake

Ingredients:
- ☐ 1 c Sugar
- ☐ 1 tb Vanilla
- ☐ 8 oz Cream cheese
- ☐ 1 c Sour cream
- ☐ 8 oz Cool Whip
- ☐ 2 Graham
- ☐ 2 cn Cherry pie filling
- ☐ Pie crusts

Directions:
Mix sugar, vanilla and cream cheese together. Stir in sour cream, then mix it slowly in blender. Add the Cool Whip.

Spread the cheese mixture evenly in graham pie crusts, then spread pie filling on top.

Chill approximately 2 hours before serving.

Simply Cheesecake

Individual Cherry Cheesecake

Ingredients:
- ☐ 2 pk Cream cheese, 8oz each
- ☐ 3/4 c Sugar
- ☐ 2 Eggs
- ☐ 1 ts Lemon juice
- ☐ 1 ts Vanilla
- ☐ 12 Vanilla wafers
- ☐ 1 cn Cherry pie filling

Directions:
Mix softened cream cheese, sugar, eggs, lemon juice and vanilla in bowl.

Place wafer in bottom of each of 12 cupcake papers (in cupcake tin).

Spoon in cream cheese mixture 3/4 full.

Bake in 375 degree oven for 15 minutes. Let cool.

Top each with cherry pie filling and refrigerate for 1 hour or more.

Simply Cheesecake

Paris Pastry Cheesecake

Ingredients:
- ☐ 3/4 c Sour cream
- ☐ 5 oz Cream cheese
- ☐ 1/2 c Sugar
- ☐ 1 Egg
- ☐ 1 8" graham cracker crust
- ☐ 1 Box strawberries
- ☐ 4 oz Whipped cream sweetened

Directions:
Place sour cream; cream cheese, sugar and egg in food processor or blender and blend until smooth. Turn into graham cracker crust and bake at 350 degrees 15 minutes.

Chill several hours, or overnight.

Garnish fruit slices and whipped cream.

Simply Cheesecake

Heavenly Orange Cheesecake

Ingredients:
Crust:
- ☐ 1 1/2 c Chocolate Wafer Crumbs
- ☐ 4 tb Unsalted Butter -- melted

Filling:
- ☐ 1 Envelope Unflavored Gelatin
- ☐ 1/2 c Orange Juice
- ☐ 24 oz Cream Cheese -- softened
- ☐ 3/4 c Sugar
- ☐ 1 c Whipping Cream -- whipped
- ☐ 2 ts Grated Orange Peel

Directions:
Combine crumbs and butter. Press onto bottom of 9-inch springform pan and bake at 350 for 10 minutes. Cool.

Soften gelatin in juice; stir over low heat until dissolved.

Combine cream cheese and sugar. Gradually add gelatin mixture.

Fold in whipped cream and peel.

Chill until firm

Simply Cheesecake

Cheeseless Cheesecake

Ingredients:
- ☐ 1 1/2 c Crushed pineapple, drained
- ☐ 1/3 c Pineapple juice, from above
- ☐ 2/3 c Dry powdered milk
- ☐ 3 pk Sweetener
- ☐ 1 tb Vanilla
- ☐ 2 Envelopes Knox gelatin
- ☐ 2 tb Lemon juice
- ☐ 1/2 c Boiling water

Directions:
In blender, blend pineapple, gelatin, water, and 1/3 cup reserved pineapple juice for 2 minutes on high speed.

Add dry milk, vanilla, and lemon juice. Blend for 2 more minutes on high.

Pour into a 9 inch pie plate.

Refrigerate until set, 2 to 3 hours.

Makes 6 servings.

Simply Cheesecake

Oh My Cheesecake

Ingredients:
- ☐ 9 Inch graham cracker crust
- ☐ 8 oz Cream cheese, soften
- ☐ 14 oz Can sweeten condensed milk
- ☐ 1/3 c Lemon juice from concentrate
- ☐ 1 ts Vanilla extract

Optional:
- ☐ 21 oz Can cherry or blueberry pie filling

Directions:
In large bowl, beat cheese until fluffy. Gradually beat in sweeten condensed milk until smooth.

Stir in lemon juice and vanilla. Pour into prepared crust.

Chill about 3 hours or until set.

Top with desired amount of pie filling before serving.

Keep chilled!

Simply Cheesecake

Little Round Cheesecakes

Ingredients:
- ☐ 8 oz Cream cheese (2)
- ☐ 3/4 c Sugar
- ☐ 2 Eggs
- ☐ 1 ts Vanilla
- ☐ Vanilla Wafers

Directions:
Put vanilla wafer in bottom of cupcake foil. Mix ingredients, Pour mixture in, bake for 15 minutes on 350.

Put in refrigerator overnight.

Add fruit before you serve.

Simply Cheesecake

Macadamia Nut Cheesecake

Ingredients:
- ☐ Prepared chocolate pie crust
- ☐ 11 oz Cream cheese
- ☐ 3/4 c Sugar
- ☐ 1 ts Vanilla
- ☐ Dash salt
- ☐ 3 Eggs
- ☐ 1/2 c Chopped macadamia nuts

Directions:
Blend cream cheese, sugar, vanilla and salt.

Add eggs one at a time. Sprinkle nuts over pie crust.

Pour filling on top.

Set on baking sheet. Bake at 325 degrees for 35 to 40 minutes. Cool.

Simply Cheesecake

Creamed Cottage Cheesecake

Ingredients:
- ☐ 1 lb Creamed cottage cheese
- ☐ 1 lb Cream cheese
- ☐ 4 Eggs, lightly beaten
- ☐ 1 1/2 tb Lemon juice
- ☐ 3 tb Cornstarch
- ☐ 3 tb Flour
- ☐ 1/4 lb Butter melted
- ☐ 1 pt Thick sour cream
- ☐ 1 Graham cracker lined pan

Directions:
Beat smooth both cheeses and beat in the eggs and vanilla to blend. Blend in lemon juice, flour and cornstarch. Add and blend in the melted butter and sour cream.

Pour into a graham cracker crumb lined pan. Bake 1 hour at 325.

Turn off oven. Let cake remain in oven with door closed for 2 hours without opening door.

Remove cake from oven and chill.

Simply Cheesecake

Cheesecake A La Chase

Ingredients:
- ☐ 1 Graham cracker crust
- ☐ 2 lb Cream cheese
- ☐ 1 1/2 c Sugar
- ☐ 4 lg Eggs
- ☐ 1 ts Vanilla
- ☐ 1/3 ts Orange rind
- ☐ 1/3 ts Lemon rind
- ☐ 1/3 c Egg whites

Directions:
Line an 8 inch springform pan with a graham cracker crust. Chill slightly.

Cream together, cream cheese and sugar. Beat in eggs one at a time. Add vanilla, orange and lemon rinds.

Fold in stiffly beaten egg whites. Pour into crust.

Bake in a preheated oven at 230 degrees F. for 2 hours and 40 minutes.

Simply Cheesecake

Miniature Cheesecakes

Ingredients:
- ☐ 16 oz Cream cheese
- ☐ 3/4 c Sugar
- ☐ 2 Eggs
- ☐ 1 ts Vanilla
- ☐ Cherry pie filling
- ☐ Vanilla wafers

Directions:
Mix cream cheese, sugar, eggs and vanilla together.

Fill muffin pan with bake cups; place vanilla wafer at bottom of each.

Fill half full of batter and bake 10 minutes or until set.

Top with pie filling.

Strawberry Cheesecake Topping

Ingredients:
- ☐ 1 tb Cornstarch
- ☐ 2 tb Orange liqueur
- ☐ 1 Unsweetened strawberries; thawed
- ☐ 1/2 c Sugar
- ☐ 1/4 c Orange juice

Directions:
Dissolve cornstarch in orange liqueur.

In pot over medium heat combine remaining ingredients. Cook until berries are very soft, 10 minutes.

Add cornstarch; cook, stirring constantly, until mixture just thickens, 3-4 minutes. Cool completely.

Makes 16 servings

Graham Cracker Cheesecake Crust

Ingredients:
- ☐ 1 1/2 c Graham Cracker Crumbs
- ☐ 1/3 c Melted Butter
- ☐ 1/3 c Sugar

Directions:
Combine all ingredients. Press into bottom and halfway up side of 9 inch springform pan.

Bake at 350 degrees for 8 to 10 minutes; cool and fill.

Cheesecake Pastry Crust

Ingredients:
- ☐ 1/3 c Softened Butter
- ☐ 1 Egg
- ☐ 1/3 c Sugar
- ☐ 1 1/4 c Unsifted Flour

Directions:
Cream butter and sugar in small mixer bowl; blend in egg.

Add flour; mix well. Spread dough on bottom and 1 1/2 inches up side of 9-inch springform pan.

Bake at 450 degrees for 5 minutes. Cool and fill.

Graham Cracker Cheesecake Crust

Ingredients:
- [ ] 1 1/2 c Graham Cracker Crumbs
- [ ] 1/3 c Sugar
- [ ] 1/3 c Melted Butter

Directions:
Mix together.

Bake at 350 degrees for 8 to 10 minutes; cool and fill.

37834316R00106

Made in the USA
Middletown, DE
13 December 2016